St

Behold, my children, the heritage I leave you:
have Charity for one another,
guard Humility,
make your treasure out of voluntary Poverty.

—St. Dominic's Last Will and Testament

St. Dominic

The Story of a Preaching Friar

DONALD J. GOERGEN, OP

Foreword by Timothy Radcliffe, OP

Paulist Press
New York / Mahwah, NJ

Library of Congress Cataloging-in-Publication Data

Names: Goergen, Donald.
Title: St. Dominic : the story of a preaching friar / Donald J. Goergen, OP ;
    foreword by Timothy Radcliffe, OP.
    Description: New York : Paulist Press, 2016. | Includes bibliographical
    references.
    Identifiers: LCCN 2015035270 (print) | LCCN 2015039682 (ebook)
  | ISBN 9780809149544 (pbk. : alk. paper) | ISBN 9781587685538 (ebook)
    Subjects: LCSH: Dominic, Saint, 1170-1221. | Saints—Spain—Biography.
    Classification: LCC BX4700.D7 G64 2016 (print) | LCC BX4700.D7
(ebook) | DDC
    271/.202—dc23
    LC record available at http://lccn.loc.gov/2015035270

ISBN 978-0-8091-4954-4 (paperback)
ISBN 978-1-58768-553-8 (e-book)

Published by Paulist Press
997 Macarthur Boulevard
Mahwah, New Jersey 07430

www.paulistpress.com

Printed and bound in the
United States of America

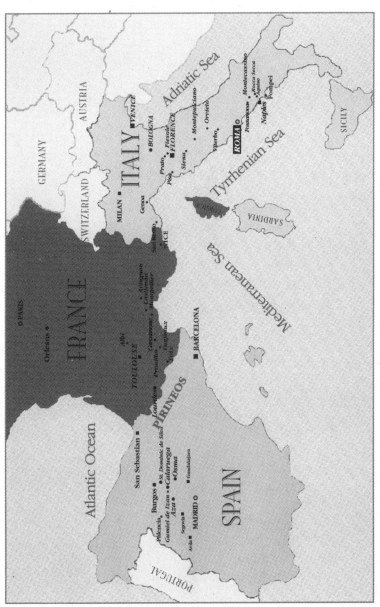

Map courtesy of John Vidmar, OP, Dominican Archives, Providence College

CONTENTS

FOREWORD

This year we celebrate the eight hundredth anniversary of the foundation of the Order of Preachers. And what better moment for a splendid new life of its founder, St. Dominic! But why are there not more lives of St. Dominic? St. Francis, his contemporary, is the subject of endless biographies. Why does Dominic receive less attention?

St. Francis wished to imitate the life of Christ, and so it is right that we look closely at him and the ways in which he was Christlike. He bore the stigmata of Christ's wounds in his body. St. Dominic was a preacher, and so he calls us to attend to the gospel rather than to himself. Preachers are like St. John the Baptist, who said, "He must increase but I must decrease" (John 3:30). The preacher must get out of the way. So it is entirely appropriate that the founder of the Order of Preachers is not the subject of endless attention. We honor him by studying the Word of the Lord. Dominic always carried with him the Gospel of Matthew and the letters of Paul, which must have weighed a lot before the invention of printing. He invites us to look at them, too.

Why, then, write a biography of Dominic? The fact that he did not draw attention to himself does not mean that he was a pale, insubstantial person, a characterless messenger. One can only be a preacher of the one who brings us abundant life if one is alive, humanly, emotionally, and spiritually. Someone who is utterly characterless could hardly point to the Lord of life. St. Dominic clearly was an attractive person of whom his brethren were very fond. Blessed Jordan of Saxony, his successor as Master of the Order, wrote that because he loved everyone, he was loved by everyone. He enjoyed the company of women and, on his deathbed, confessed that he enjoyed talking with young women more than being talked at by old women! Surely he laughed when he said this!

These early brethren were obviously warm and humane people. Jordan writes of his friendship for Henry, Prior of Cologne: "My dearest friend in Christ. I loved him more than anyone else in the world. He really was a vessel of honor and grace. I do not remember ever seeing any more gracious creature in this life." Jordan wrote some of the most beautiful and tender letters of the Middle Ages to his beloved Blessed Diana d'Andalò. There was no fear of "particular friendships."

St. Dominic was an ascetic who enjoyed his wine. It is no coincidence that his mission began in an inn! The dominant metaphor for the gospel in the first centuries of the Order was "the new wine." He pointed to the Lord in part by being the humane person God called him to be, by being the unique word that God has spoken in and through his being. It is preachers who are not easy in their skin, uncomfortable in their humanity, who drag our attention toward themselves and distract us from the gospel.

Another reason why there have not been many biographies of St. Dominic is because he never wanted to be seen as the great Founder, but as one of the brethren. Much of our information about his life comes from an early book called, appropriately, *Vitae Fratrum*, "The lives of the brethren." The preaching of the gospel is rooted in our fraternal life. Dominican brethren are formed to speak the Word of God by the discipline of living with, loving, and forgiving one another. How can one speak of the God who is love if one cannot love the person in the room next door?

It is always tempting for the preacher to want to become a star. One of the early brethren who had a tremendous success as a preacher was irritated that when he had his hair cut, the brethren did not rush forward to collect the clippings! Dominic wanted the brethren to be sent to preach two by two, pointing beyond themselves to the Lord.

It is appropriate that the foundation of the Order of Preachers was not the project of a single man, imposed on his followers. St. Dominic first discovered his mission when he was the companion of his bishop, Diego. Who knows whether it was Dominic or Diego who first had the idea of a band of preachers? Maybe it emerged from their conversations on the road. I learned from this biography that the choice of the Rule of St. Augustine was probably made by the brethren, rather than just by Dominic. Also it is argued convincingly that it was Pope Innocent III who may have had the idea of an Order of Preachers with a universal mission, rather than a little local community based in the south of France. So the Order was born of multiple conversations. Dominic was the focal point of conversations with the pope, with Diego his bishop, with the nuns at Prouilhe, and with the early brethren. He listened attentively to other people's ideas. His genius was to be the midwife of a new way of religious life by being open to the ideas and intuitions of others.

The preacher is, in the first place, someone who listens: to God, to the scriptures, to the Church, to the brethren and sisters, and to anyone who has a word they need to speak. We have nothing to say until we have listened. If we do not listen, then we shall impose our agenda on people rather than wisdom of the Lord.

This discipline of mutual attention is embodied in St. Dominic's form of government, in which we gather together in chapter to make decisions about our common life and our mission. The spirituality of Dominic is, surprisingly for many, embodied in this democracy. Of course, Dominic lived in a time when democracy, in many forms, was in the air; 1215 was the year of the proclamation of the Magna Carta in England. Dominican democracy, however, is much more than an effective way of government. It sustains and depends upon the fraternal life that underpins our preaching. Each brother and sister is given something to say by the Lord.

A final point: Don Goergen stresses that Dominic was a contemplative itinerant preacher. He was always on the road, crossing and recrossing Europe, preaching the gospel, and visiting his brethren and the nuns. And yet at the center of his life was contemplative silence, which opened him to God and to those whom he met on the road. Dominic shows us that the contemplative life does not demand that we retreat from the world, behind the walls of enclosed monasteries. It was possible in the midst of the vibrant bustle of thirteenth-century Europe, with its new cities and universities, its new trade and intellectual life, its rediscovery of ancient Greek learning and dialogue with Islam.

This is a challenge for us eight hundred years later. We are busier than ever, endless in communication through phone and computer, ever rushing from one place to another by car and plane. Dominic invites us to discover how we can be still and contemplative in this frenetic global village. Otherwise, we shall not be able to offer anything nourishing to our contemporaries who are so hungry and thirsty for a word of life.

Timothy Radcliffe, OP

PREFACE

⸺∞⸺

Dominic is a saint. That much is clear. Sometimes that fact can obscure how difficult it is to know someone from the inside out, so to speak. We confine our understanding to historically determinable facts. But this does little to bring someone, especially a saint, to life—there is more to the story of a saint than historical facts alone. My desire here is not so much to write a life of Dominic but to bring him to life. While desiring to be as faithful as I can to the historical data available to us, I have nevertheless had to interpret the data, even what I might choose to emphasize. I have attempted a balance between the historical and the interpretative, knowing that the former without the latter betrays what history itself is, or pretends an objectivity unavailable to us, while the latter without the former can lead to a purely personal report that will be corrected by the facts themselves.

With the life of Dominic, it is not always easy to ascertain the facts. We do the best we can. Some things are well established and well documented. Many others require sifting, prudent judgments, and at times, reasoned hypotheses that every historian must readily make. We often know more about who a person is after they have died and can look back at a life with hindsight. There is more than what a fact might originally have suggested. Imagination itself has to be given a proper place in reconstruction. What God asks of us is not always what we have ourselves chosen, and what God makes of us goes beyond what we ourselves have done. This is particularly true of the life of a saint. There is always more to the story than what meets the eye.

Deeply grounded in the Lord, Dominic was a person who sustained a remarkably contemplative equanimity in the face of the challenges life brought his way. He trusted God as governing the universe providentially with wisdom and love. He saw grace in all things. Gratitude, or joy, was characteristic of him, as was humility, the other side of the coin of gratitude. In his so-called last will to his followers, his brothers and sisters, he enjoined upon them to be humble. He was loved, and he knew himself to be loved, both by God and by friends whom he wove into the fabric of his life. But this is beginning to paint the portrait, or tell the story, too soon.

So let me first take a moment to express gratitude myself, to Nancy de Flon, my gracious editor at Paulist Press, who had faith in this project when I first proposed it; to Barbara Beaumont, OP, of the Association of Sister Historians of the Order of Preachers, whose help was always reassuring; to Simon Tugwell, OP, for his indefatigable commitment to research; to Stan Drongowski, OP, for his initial reading and helpful editing of the manuscript; and to Timothy Radcliffe, OP, for providing the foreword in the midst of a very busy schedule. I also wish to thank my sisters, Janet and Judy, for their constant support throughout my life, as well as my Dominican brothers and sisters, without whom I would not have come to know my brother Dominic. They are my family too and among them are some of my closest friends. There are many to whom I am deeply grateful for their encouragement, friendship, and wisdom, all of whom I cannot name here but who certainly know who they are. Thank you.

Donald J. Goergen, OP

A Brief Chronology

ca. 1172–1174   Dominic is born in Caleruega, in Old Castile, present-day Spain.

ca. 1186/1187   Dominic goes to study the liberal arts, philosophy, and theology in Palencia.

ca. 1197/1198   Dominic joins the cathedral chapter of canons in Osma.

1201 (by January 13)   Dominic is subprior of the cathedral chapter in Osma.

1203–1204   Dominic makes his first journey with Bishop Diego to the north to arrange a royal wedding for the king of Castile.

1205   Dominic and Diego leave late in the year for their second journey to the north on behalf of the king of Castile.

1206   Diego and Dominic meet the three Cistercian papal legates in Montpellier early in the year.

1206–1207   Diego and Dominic establish a home for converted Cathar women in Prouilhe, probably in late 1206.

1207   Dominic and Diego participate in a formal debate with the Cathars in Montréal in late March. Later in the year, Diego, and possibly Dominic, participate in another debate at Pamiers. The papal legate, Raoul, dies in early July.

1207 (December 30)	Bishop Diego dies in Osma.
1208 (January 14)	Peter of Castelnau, a papal legate, is assassinated.
1208 (March 10)	Pope Innocent III calls for a crusade. Dominic, at some point, returns or had returned to Osma.
1209 (July 22)	The beginning of the crusade with the massacre at Béziers.
1211	Dominic is back in Languedoc, after having spent the years following the death of Diego in Osma, and is in charge of the community at Prouilhe.
1212	Dominic spends time in Prouilhe. In December, he is elected bishop of Béziers but refused to accept.
1213	Dominic preaches a Lenten cycle at the cathedral in Carcassonne.
1214	Dominic ministers in Fanjeaux, Prouilhe, Carcassonne, and Toulouse. The papal legate, Peter of Benevento, officially appoints Dominic the head of the *praedicatio* (preaching).
1215	Peter Seilhan and Thomas pledge themselves to Dominic as his associates in the preaching. Dominic establishes a diocesan preaching institute in Toulouse.
1215 (April 25)	Peter Seilhan turns a house, his portion of an inheritance, over to Dominic.
1215 (October–December)	Dominic and Bishop Fulk of Toulouse are in Rome on the occasion of the Fourth Lateran Council and confer with Pope Innocent III about the preaching. Pope Innocent encourages Dominic to form a religious community.
1216 (summer)	Dominic and his brethren choose the Rule of St. Augustine.
1216 (July 16)	Pope Innocent III dies.

1216 (July 18)	Cencio Savelli becomes Pope Honorius III.
1216 (December 22)	Pope Honorius III confirms Dominic and his brethren as a religious institute. Dominic has returned to Rome by this time.
1217 (January 21)	Pope Honorius III confirms preaching as the goal of Dominic's order and acknowledges them as *praedicatores* (Preachers). Later, Dominic accepts William of Montferrat into the Order and sends him to Paris for study.
1217 (August 15)	Dominic disperses his brethren to Paris and to Spain.
1218 (early)	Pope Honorius III explicitly designates the Order as the Order of Preachers. From Rome, Dominic sends some brothers to Bologna. Dominic receives Reginald of Orléans into the Order and sends him to Bologna as well.
1218 (summer)	Dominic goes from Rome to Spain and visits Madrid and Segovia.
1219	Dominic goes from Spain to Paris via Toulouse and then to Bologna, arriving in Bologna with William of Montferrat not before August 15. He later receives the profession of Diana d'Andalò.
1219 (November)	Dominic is at the papal court in Viterbo and accepts the commission to reform the Roman nuns within a new monastery at San Sisto.
1220	Dominic is in Viterbo, Rome, and Bologna.
1220 (May 20)	The first General Chapter of the Order in Bologna.
1221 (February 28)	Dominic establishes the monastery at San Sisto in Rome. Previously, Pope Honorius III had given Santa Sabina to Dominic to accommodate the friars.

1221 (June 2)	The second General Chapter of the Order in Bologna.
1221 (August 6)	Dominic dies in Bologna.
1234 (July 3)	Dominic is canonized by Pope Gregory IX.

CHAPTER 1

What's in a Name?

I had never met a Dominican priest until I went off to college. I had never actually met a religious priest; all those I knew were diocesan men in the Diocese of Sioux City, Iowa. Franciscan sisters from Dubuque, Iowa, taught me in both grade school and high school. They were and remain some of the best teachers I have ever had. As for religious men, I had heard or read about them. I remember seeing pictures of some in books as I pondered a priestly vocation already in eighth grade. But dad insisted that we had a good Catholic high school right there in Remsen, and there was no need to leave that school for a high school seminary education. I was only in eighth grade, after all. So I waited four more years and then joined the diocese since I was familiar with others from my hometown who had gone on to the priesthood and studied for the diocese. I went to college in a preseminary track where Dominicans taught philosophy. I liked philosophy and I liked my teachers; some were diocesan priests; some were members of the Order of Preachers. I still knew little about Dominic at the time. I majored in Latin and in philosophy.

One's life unfolds, but seldom in accord with one's plans. Nevertheless, providence is always at work. After some major illnesses in my family and a hesitant moment on the part of my bishop, I went on to major seminary. It was an exciting moment in history. The Second Vatican Council had begun while I was in college, and in 1965, we were beginning to see its welcome effects. A spirit of freer thinking, one might even say rebellion, permeated the traditional seminary milieu. While I lived in the diocesan seminary, we took our classes in theology at the Aquinas Institute, sponsored and staffed by Dominicans. I saw what it meant to have a call to be both priest and teacher. However, I was expelled from the diocesan seminary in my third year of theology. After growth-filled experiences apart from seminary life, and following what was probably a perfunctory investigation of various religious orders, the handwriting was on the wall: I had more experience with and more support from the Dominican friar professors than from anywhere else. It was providential. I professed my first vows in December of 1971.

All of the above is only meant to introduce the man I grew to know and love: St. Dominic de Guzmán. It is his story, not mine, that I wish to tell, although they are always intertwined. It is within my own story that his came alive. There are several scholarly books to which I can refer you, at different levels of comprehensiveness, all worth your further study. I do not intend to repeat what they have so well done.[1] As Edward Schillebeeckx, an eminent twentieth-century Flemish Dominican suggested, the Dominican story is only kept alive by live

---

1. A scholarly and comprehensive treatment remains that of M.-H. Vicaire, OP, *Saint Dominic and His Times*, trans. Kathleen Pond, a translation of the first edition (New York: McGraw-Hill, 1964), reprinted by Alt Publishing Co., Green Bay, Wisconsin. The most recent historical research can be found in Simon Tugwell, OP, "Notes on the life of St. Dominic," in varied volumes of the *Archivum Fratrum Praedicatorum* (abbr. *AFP*), published by the Dominican Historical Institute, Rome. A very competent and highly recommended shorter work is that by Vladimir Koudelka, OP, *Dominic*, trans. and ed. Consuelo Fissler, OP, and Simon Tugwell, OP (London: Darton, Longman and Todd, 1997). There are also the works of Guy Bedouelle, OP, and William A. Hinnebusch, OP, among others.

Dominicans.[2] It is through them that we come to know Dominic and that is how I first came to know him, through what has come to be recognized as a Dominican family. Dominic was a friar and a preacher, and he wanted his order, once he was guided to found one, to be an order of preachers, not the Order of St. Dominic. His vocation in life was to be a preaching friar.

Names can be prescient. This is why at Baptism the names we are given are significant. This is why many religious have taken, and frequently continue to take, a new name when incorporated into a religious family. I did not take a religious name. My paternal grandfather's name was Dominic Goergen; my paternal grandmother's name was Catherine Meyer. While growing up on a farm, my paternal grandparents' names were seldom mentioned as they had been long deceased. My grandfather died when dad was nine. His mother died when he was fourteen. Evidently, dad wanted to name me Dominic after his father, but my mother hesitated. So I was named Donald Joseph (Joseph after dad's brother-in-law), but somehow underneath it all, Dominic lurked in the background. I did not know the story about my naming until dad died and my aunt told the story. So, growing up, Dominic was only in the background. I knew little about him.

How St. Dominic himself got his name is also a story, more story than history perhaps. In Old Castile (Spain), not far from Caleruega where Dominic was born, was the town of Silos. In Silos is a Benedictine monastery that houses the remains of a locally famous eleventh-century Spanish saint who died in 1073, Santo Domingo de Silos. He is, among other things, the patron saint of pregnant women, and the monastery had been renamed

---

2. Edward Schillebeeckx, OP, "Dominican Spirituality," in *God among Us, the Gospel Proclaimed*, trans. John Bowden (New York: Crossroad, 1983), 232–48.

for him.[3] It was to his shrine that Jane (or Juana), Dominic's mother, made a pilgrimage to pray to the holy saint for a safe pregnancy. Jordan of Saxony records a dream or vision of Jane's.[4] Whether she had it at the shrine or not, it is associated with her prayer to the renowned saint. She saw herself with a little dog in her womb, with a blazing torch in its mouth, who set the world on fire upon being born. It was interpreted for her: she would give birth to a son whose resounding voice would be heard throughout the world. She named her son Dominic after the Benedictine saint whose intercession she had sought in her prayer. The Latin word for Dominicans, *Dominicani*, also says *Domini canes*, which translated means "dogs of the Lord." This gave great word play in medieval times: hounds of heaven if you will. What's in a name? The Dominican Dominic, in time, superseded in fame his Benedictine namesake, although the monastery in Silos remains to this day. It has often led me to say that inside every Dominican, there is something Benedictine. Even Dominic's order had its origins in monastic traditions, even if a friar is not the same thing as a monk. So what is a friar?

FRIAR

There are monastic orders, such as Benedictines and Cistercians, and their members are called monks or nuns. There is

---

3. Evidently, until 1931, it was the custom for the abbot to leave the staff of St. Dominic of Silos at the bedside of the queen of Spain during childbirth.

4. Jordan of Saxony, *Libellus*, #5. See Jordan of Saxony, *On the Beginnings of the Order of Preachers*, trans. Simon Tugwell, OP (Dublin: Dominican Publications, 1982), 31n1. Future references to the *Libellus* are to this translation and will be indicated within the text by paragraph numbers. Vicaire, p. 21, notes that a similar story can be found in reference to earlier saints as well. Jordan was the friar to succeed Dominic as Master of the Order, thus its second Master. His *Libellus*, whose final composition is dated 1232–33, is the earliest account we have of St. Dominic and the early history of the Order. On its composition and date, see Tugwell, *AFP* 68 (1998): 5–33, esp. 32–33.

supposed to be an element of stability in their lives, and their houses or abbeys are to provide a sense of withdrawal from the world. When Dominic established his order of preaching friars, he did not want them confined in an enclosed setting according to the character of monastic life at the time. He wanted to send them out, and send them out he did, to preach the gospel and to teach the truth of the Catholic faith. They would be both itinerant and mendicant—a novel form of religious life indeed. They would not be living in self-supported or well-endowed abbeys, and their lives were intended to be lived on the road as much as in a cloister. Thus a new movement had begun, a new moment in the history of religious life. There were now friars as well as monks.

The Dominicans were not the only friars. The Franciscan friars were founded by Francis of Assisi at about the same time. Both were new, maligned, and vibrant orders, and they grew rapidly. But we are getting ahead of ourselves, for Dominic did not found his order until 1216. He was born shortly after 1170. We need to come back soon to his story. But it is important to remember what Dominic became, a friar, and that he is remembered today as a preacher. There are monastic orders, and orders primarily apostolic or active—many of which were founded after the Reformation, but Thomas Aquinas, as well known a Dominican as Dominic himself, spoke about the friar Preachers as being a mixture of both. They are a mix indeed, deeply contemplative, yet itinerant and apostolic, defined by their mission. Grounded in contemplative living, they hand on the Word of God to others. As Thomas put it in his *Summa Theologiae*, *contemplata aliis tradere*.[5]

---

5. St. Thomas Aquinas, *Summa Theologiae*, II–II (the *Secunda Secundae*), questions 186–88 on religious life, and in q. 188, article 6, one reads, "For even as it is better to enlighten than merely to shine, so it is better to give to others the fruits of one's contemplation than merely to contemplate." Texts from the *Summa* are from the translation by the Fathers of the English Dominican Province (New York: Benziger Brothers, 1947).

To contemplate and to hand on to others the fruits of one's con-templation—*contemplari et contemplata aliis tradere*—later became one of the three mottos of the Order. But that "handing on"—*tradere*—brings us to another word: *preacher*.

PREACHER

Aristotle said in his *Metaphysics* that "to be" can be said or understood in many ways.[6] We can likewise say that preaching can have more than one meaning. For many, it is a turnoff, for others a disappointment. But at its heart, it is really good news. In the Christian tradition, it is often accompanied by the *gospel*, another multivalent word. What did Dominic mean when he wanted his order to be an order of preachers? What was he doing when he and his bishop, Diego, "preached" in southern France? What did he understand when he would sign a document *praedicationis humilis minister* (humble servant of preaching)?[7] How was his desire to present the truth of the Catholic faith to Cathars—the heretical movement that arose in the church in the eleventh century[8]—"preaching"? It had something to do with truth, another motto of the Order: *veritas*. It also had to do with a bold-ness or fearlessness in engaging others in that quest for truth. It was not simply something confined to a pulpit, although it could take place there as well; or, as a friend of mine has said, the Order is an order of preachers, not an order of homilists. Dominic's preaching had everything to do with Jesus Christ, "to proclaim

---

6. Aristotle, *Metaphysics*, bk. 4, chap. 2; also bk. 7, chap. 1.

7. Latin texts at this time often spell preaching as *predicatio*. For the sake of consistency with a later spelling, however, I will write *praedicatio*.

8. The Cathars are also called Albigensians after the city of Albi in southern France where many of them were clustered.

Christ Jesus and Him crucified," as St. Paul the preacher and Apostle said (1 Cor 1:23; 2:2).

Dominic's mission became more and more apostolic or evangelical. One might say it required the kind of life lived by the apostles (the *vita apostolica*).[9] It was grounded in the gospel (the *evangelium*) and put at the service of those needing a saving word in their lives and seeking salvation. To be a preacher was to mediate God's Word in human words: a word of love, mercy, and compassion. Mercy (*misericordia*), truth (*veritas*), and brotherhood (*fraternitas*), or the *vita communis*—the common life —were all sacred words for Dominic, that man of the Lord who was filled with God. He became known as a *praedicator gratiae*, a preacher of grace and a grace-filled preacher. The story has also been handed on how Dominic, while a young student in Palencia, when there was a famine in the region, sold his parchments or manuscripts that he so dearly treasured in order to provide some funding for the poor and the hungry. He said, "I will not study on dead skins when living skins are dying of hunger." Evidently, we find the rudiments of Dominic's character manifest early in his life. Whether it was in response to a hunger for food or thirst for truth, our preaching friar was there. The time has come to take a closer look at the man.

---

9. On the developing understanding of the apostolic life in the twelfth and thirteenth centuries, see M.-D. Chenu, "Monks, Canons, and Laymen in Search of the Apostolic Life," in *Nature, Man and Society in the Twelfth Century* (Chicago: University of Chicago Press, 1968), 202–38.

CHAPTER 2

EARLY FORMATION, 1170–1206

THE TIME: LATE TWELFTH CENTURY; THE PLACE: OLD CASTILE, OR SPAIN; THE TOWN: CALERUEGA

Caleruega, with its long winters, is still there today, as bleak and beautiful as ever, as any small village in the country might be. Unlike many of his followers today, Dominic was not an urban man. Sheep and shepherds were at home in Caleruega as much as the villagers were themselves. Having grown up on a farm myself, in Plymouth County, Iowa, and having visited Caleruega on several occasions, as well as the Duchy of Luxembourg from which my paternal great grandparents came, I can appreciate several things that were formative of Dominic's character: being at ease with solitude, the centrality of the parish church, solace found in books along with a desire for learning, an appreciation of family life as well as the natural world. God looms everywhere. Manmade architecture does not blur the horizon. The steeple or tower of the parish church marks the town and dedicates it to God. There is room for the Spirit to breathe. Life and its sustenance depend on the weather and the providence of God.

Dominic's parents were Felix and Jane. He was reported to be from Guzmán, she from Aza, both within a twenty- to thirty-mile radius from Caleruega, although historians today recommend silence with respect to Dominic's genealogy as there is insufficient evidence that he was a descendent of the Guzmán and the Aza.[1] Felix and Jane, however, were the names of his parents. They were married in 1170. Dominic's father does not seem to have been wealthy but, nevertheless, was of a noble background. His father traveled and Dominic spent more time with his mom—from whom he evidently learned many things, some of the most significant things in life. She must have felt close to him, fond, even protective, considering the dream she had had during the pregnancy, which would have led Dominic's mother to ponder many things in her heart (see Luke 2:51). Jane is reported to have had a heart for the poor, "full of compassion toward the unfortunate and those in distress," as an early account described her.[2] When her husband was away, the poor would come to her door. On at least one occasion, she evidently distributed valued wine from their cask in the cellar to the point of having emptied it while her husband was away. Upon his return, thirsty, asking for some wine, what was she to do? Going to the wine cellar, she found, following upon her prayer, that the cask had been miraculously replenished, much to her relief, and perhaps even disbelief. Some of her kindness rubbed off on her son, who later, as we have said, sold his books to help the poor. He could perhaps sense

---

1. Vicaire accepted the tradition that Dominic's mother was d'Aza and his father de Guzmán, pp. 16–18, 403–07, but Tugwell points to the lack of evidence in this regard and suggests that Vicaire may have been rethinking this himself. See Simon Tugwell, OP, "Notes on the life of St. Dominic," in *Archivum Fratrum Praedicatorum* (AFP) 67 (1997): 57–59.

2. Vicaire, *St. Dominic*, 18, following a description by Rodríguez de Cerrato writing in the late thirteenth century.

his mom's presence, or gentle pressure, certainly her example, on occasions like that.

Dominic had two older brothers, Antony and Mamés. Dominic himself was born in 1173 or 1174; the dating cannot be precise. Antony was a priest who gave himself to works of mercy in hospices devoted to hospitality for the poor—again the influence of Jane makes itself felt in another of the sons. Some have suggested that Mamés was a half-brother,[3] Jane's son from a previous marriage. But it seems more historically reliable to say that Felix was Jane's only husband and that all Dominic's siblings were the children of both parents.[4] Mamés later joined the Order and became a preaching friar himself. He was still alive at the time of Dominic's canonization in 1234. Dominic sent him on his first mission, which was back to his native land, his beloved Spain.

Late eleventh- and early twelfth-century Spain was not as we know it today. The southern region, Andalusia, was still primarily Muslim, whereas the northern area of Castile was Catholic, since the "Moors" had been pushed back from northern Spain, especially with the reconquest of Toledo in 1085. There was still tension and conflict between Christians and Muslims, who at a later date, lived in peace with each other, since all this took place almost three centuries before the Catholic monarchs, Ferdinand and Isabella, and the expulsion of Jews from Spain and before the "Moors" were driven from Spain as well.

Dominic's milieu was Catholic and so was his education. The font in which he was baptized can be viewed even today, although it is no longer located in the little Romanesque church in Caleruega, a church that Dominic himself would have known and that had been constructed not so long before his birth. The

---

3. Vicaire, St. *Dominic*, 19–20.
4. See Tugwell, *AFP* 67 (1996): 27–34.

foundations of the font are there in the parish church in Caleruega, although the font itself is now in Madrid. One can also view in Caleruega the *torreón* or old tower close to the probable place of Dominic's birth. When Mamés returned to "Spain," there was already an established monastery of Dominican nuns in Madrid to whom he ministered. Dominic himself had a special care for women. His first establishment, even before there was an Order, was for converted Cathar women for whom he and Bishop Diego provided a residence in Prouilhe,[5] on which site even today there stands an international community of Dominican nuns. Dominic had this "family spirit" from the beginning—perhaps his mom's influence again. She was obviously a prayerful woman. Who would make a pilgrimage while pregnant? The countryside around Caleruega was rugged and Silos was not close, only close by modern standards.

FROM CALERUEGA TO PALENCIA

If Dominic were to receive a clerical as well as a liberal education, the questions would be where to go and how to be prepared? Not in Caleruega. Instead, the question was to whom to entrust this child's care as well as to prepare him for a university style education? Here an uncle, a priest, enters the scene. He, or one of the priests associated with his uncle's church, provided the young Dominic with what he needed to be prepared for the liberal arts that he would then pursue in a genuine center of learning, namely, Palencia, the intellectual center of Castile. An actual university was formally established in

---

5. *Prouille* is the French spelling, *Prouilhe* is the Occitan form, a language spoken in Catalonia. Being in the Languedoc, Prouilhe was not a French-speaking monastery until the seventeenth century when Louis XIV sought to impose national standardization.

Palencia around 1212, which was the first university in Spain, although Salamanca soon superseded it in reputation. But the fact that it was the first Spanish university, following the pattern of what was developing in Paris and Bologna, is testimony to the quality of its education even prior to the formal establishment.

Dominic left for Palencia after five or six years under the tutelage of his priest-uncle, around the age of thirteen or fourteen, not an unusual age at that time for proceeding to liberal studies. One can only sense Dominic's eagerness to learn, his curiosity about God and the world, a fine mind at work and disciplined by a virtuous studiousness. One cannot determine precisely what his course of studies may have been, but it probably included the seven arts of the classical *trivium* (grammar, logic, and rhetoric) and *quadrivium* (arithmetic, geometry, music, and astronomy), after which he would have moved on to philosophy (natural philosophy or physics as well as metaphysics) and then theology, which would have been Dominic's major interest. Jordan of Saxony writes in his *Libellus*:

> Afterwards he was sent to Palencia to be formed in the liberal arts, because there was a thriving arts faculty there at this time. When he thought he had learned enough of the arts, he abandoned them and fled to the study of theology, as if he was afraid to waste his limited time on less fruitful study. He began to develop a passionate appetite for God's words, finding them "sweeter than honey to his mouth." (no. 6)

Dominic's vocation to the priesthood seems to have already been settled in Caleruega. Would Dominic's mother have shared with him any of the things she experienced in her dream or had she too pondered all of that quietly in her heart? Apart from a mother's reticence to share such things with her son, he had become conscious early on of his desire or destiny to serve the Church, and then it was even more nourished by his priest-uncle and his study of theology. His study was for no earthly gain. At this point in his life, he was already inclined to speak only of God or with God, as he would later instruct his brothers in the Order to do, one of the few instructions of Dominic himself that has come down to us in the tradition.[6]

It was while in Palencia that the famine took place during which Dominic experienced the urgency for the corporal works of mercy and set up a center of charity, letting go of his own possessions. He sold his books or, better said, parchments or manuscripts, and is reported as having said, "How can I keep these dead skins when living skins are dying of hunger?" He had his mother's sensitivity for the poor. But what comes after this university-style education and the training in theology that he had pursued? Spending ten or eleven years in Palencia, having gone there around 1186 or 1187, Dominic left for Osma, the cathedral city of the diocese, in 1197 or 1198.

FROM PALENCIA TO OSMA

We thus find our young man around the age of twenty-four or twenty-five joining the cathedral chapter of canons in Osma, who followed the Rule of St. Augustine in living "the regular life."

---

6. Speaking *cum Deo vel de Deo* (with God or of God) is an expression contained in the Primitive Constitutions of the Order (no. 31). The same expression is also ascribed to Stephen of Muret (1045–1124), the founder of the Abbey of Grandmont. The Bologna canonization process for St. Dominic interprets the phrase as descriptive of Dominic and as instructive for his brothers. Also see Tugwell, AFP 66 (1996): 71–72.

Canons

Canons or canons regular were ordinarily diocesan priests—priests attached to a diocese and under the authority of the local bishop. Cathedral canons lived in community, shared property in common, took a vow of stability, and often followed a rule, and thus lived a semi-monastic or "regular life" (meaning that they followed a rule or *regula*). Although they were secular clergy, the life of a canon resembled religious life in many ways. In contrast to the monastic life of cloistered religious, the life of a canon was clearly clerical and comprised public ministry. A chapter of canons comprised the diocesan clergy at the service of the cathedral and the bishop who presided over the chapter.

There is evidence that by August of 1199, he had already been appointed sacristan, a position that held great significance in terms of the liturgical life of the community.[7] The bishop of Osma at the time Dominic joined the chapter was Martín Bazán (bishop from 1189–1201) and the prior of the chapter was Diego de Acebo, who succeeded Martín as the bishop (1201–8). By that time, Dominic was already the subprior of the cathedral chapter. Of Diego, Jordan of Saxony writes,

> If any of [Diego's] subjects were sluggish in their desire
> for holiness, being more interested in worldly things,
> he urged them in words and inspired them by his exam-
> ple to adopt a more commendable pattern of behavior

---

7. We do not know precisely when and where Dominic was ordained to the priesthood, whether before or after joining the cathedral chapter.

and a more serious form of religious life. As part of this program, he did his best, by means of frequent exhortations and unceasing encouragement, to persuade his canons to agree to follow the Rule of St. Augustine and to live as canons regular, and, as a result of his efforts, he succeeded in winning their minds to his purpose, though some of them resisted him. (*Libellus*, no. 4)

As was common for many cathedral chapters, the chapter in Osma followed the Rule of St. Augustine and had recently returned to a strict observance of it. A reading of the rule, which

---

Rule of St. Augustine

A rule is drawn up to guide a celibate, monastic, or religious way of life within the Church. Perhaps best known in the Western world is the Rule of St. Benedict. Another rule, different from and probably earlier than the Rule of St. Benedict, was the Rule of St. Augustine. Some scholars question how much of it is to be attributed to Augustine himself. St. Augustine (354–430), as bishop of Hippo in North Africa (396–430), desired that his priests live a more common and rigorous life. The rule was a guideline for them. It became widely used and was adapted in the late eleventh and early twelfth century as a way of life for the canons. It permitted active ministry, as it was designed for priests, but a life of ministry grounded in the contemplative life. The basis of the Rule of St. Augustine is the evangelical principle found in the Acts of the Apostles (4:32): "Now the whole group of those who believed were of one heart and soul, and no one claimed private ownership of any possessions, but everything they owned was held in common."

is fewer than ten pages in a modern translation, would be a good entry point for appreciating the life that Dominic lived in Osma as well as for the life of the preaching friars as later formed by Dominic.[8] As a flexible program of observances for living the common life, it had the possibility of wide application, which is why Dominic and his brothers later chose it to guide their beginnings as well. In addition to the observances of the common life, Jordan reports on Dominic's life of intense personal prayer, including his deep affection for the Conferences of John Cassian, which he kept by his bedside (*Libellus*, no. 13).[9]

More remained in store for Dominic's formation, however. He seems to have been a gifted, grace-filled, respected young man. Before long, he had found himself with the position of sacristan, which was not how we understand sacristans today: ultimately responsible for "things" in the sacristies, yes, but more so responsible for the liturgical life of the community—an overseer of a community's life of prayer. No small privilege indeed when one considers Dominic's age and the importance of common prayer as well as personal prayer in the life of a cathedral canon. Soon he became subprior. Dominic clearly had the trust and respect of the superior of the community, a trust and respect also manifested by his bishop. For, while Dominic must have chosen the life of a canon because of a certain appeal for a more contemplative life, the bishop could see in him the promise of other things as well. This is why Bishop Diego invited Dominic

---

8. An excellent reflection on the Rule of St. Augustine are the retreat conferences of Walter Wagner, OP, *Dominican Life, a Commentary on the Rule of Saint Augustine*, published by the Dominican Nuns of the Perpetual Rosary, Summit, New Jersey. Also see Augustine of Hippo, *Selected Writings*, ed. Mary Clark, The Classics of Western Spirituality (New York: Paulist Press, 1984), 481–93.

9. John Cassian, *The Conferences*, trans. and ed. Boniface Ramsey, OP (New York: Paulist Press, 1997).

to accompany him on an arduous, long, and important journey that he was to make to northern Europe on behalf of King Alfonso VIII, the king of Castile. Dominic had spent about ten

---

King Alfonso VIII

Alfonso VIII (1155–1214) was King of Castile and particularly remembered for his role in the *Reconquista*, the reconquest of Spain from Muslim domination, and the rising supremacy therefore of Castile. In 1203, he wished to arrange a marriage for his thirteen-year-old son, Ferdinand, to a young noblewoman in the area of Scandinavia, and he entrusted this mission to the bishop of Osma. Ferdinand was young, but this was not uncommon at the time. Blanche of Castile, Ferdinand's sister, was married to Louis VIII of France when they were twelve, and Alfonso himself had been married at the age of fifteen to Eleanor, the daughter of Eleanor of Aquitaine.

---

or eleven years in his courses of study in Palencia, but only lived the life of a canon in Osma for five or six years before his life would shift dramatically. Nevertheless, these years were formative of the contemplative life in which he would remain grounded for the rest of his life.

DOMINIC ENCOUNTERS A HERESY

In 1203, Bishop Diego was to help arrange for a marriage between the king's son and a young woman in the region of present-day Scandinavia, probably Denmark. This does not sound like episcopal business, but in those days, the distinction between church and state was not so forcefully delineated as in our own times. The Catholic bishop was the ideal person to perform this service for the king. He would only be absent from his diocese for a time, although a sufficiently lengthy one. As a companion or *socius*, the bishop chose Dominic—a congenial, holy, and intelligent companion who must have manifested some diplomatic sensibilities of his own, whom Diego knew and probably had recruited for the cathedral chapter in Osma when Diego was its prior. For the first time, Dominic ventured outside his native land. The bishop and his entourage—including soldiers, servants, and an interpreter—left Osma by the end of May 1203. Along the way, having crossed the Pyrenees, they stopped in Toulouse, a region deeply infected by the Cathar heresy.

Dominic's docility in response to the privilege of accompanying the bishop did not anticipate what he was to find outside Catholic Spain—a heretical Church. Dominic would have known of Jews and Muslims with whom there had been both peace and war for years back in Castile. Calling oneself a Christian without remaining faithful to the Church or its teachings would have been a disturbing novelty. They were more of a parallel church. They had been ordaining their own bishops and had their own episcopal sees throughout southern France, in the region of the *langue d'oc*, as well as in northern Italy. They were Cathars, or Albigensians, latter-day Manicheans, radical cosmological as well as ontological dualists.

THE CATHARS

The Cathars, or Albigensians (a name given to the Cathars of southern France due to their strong association with the city of Albi), had first become an organized church of its own in the

Languedoc in 1167, when Cathar bishops were appointed for Toulouse and Carcassonne as well as for Albi.[10] Although there were many varied and diverse sects of Cathars, especially in northern Italy, they all held the Manichaean belief that matter and everything associated with it was just plain evil. On the one hand, it can be easy to see how they may have come by that. St. Augustine himself was drawn into Manichaeism early in his life. At first it may seem a satisfying solution to the perplexing and perennial "problem" of evil. Simply put: there must be an evil god as well as a good God—two ultimate metaphysical principles that explain the world and are so very much tied into our own destinies. Cathars sought a kind of rigorous asceticism that, from a Catholic point of view, was demeaning of God because it demeaned God's creation. Cathars didn't believe that a good God would create a material world so unlike the Spirit that God is. There were thus "two Gods," the God of the Old Testament—the Creator God—and the God of the New Testament, the God of all goodness. Creation was the work of the evil god, and all things connected with it must be given distance. The Christ of the New Testament was pure spirit, and his incarnation was illusory.

Cathars viewed the Roman Church as the "synagogue of Satan" and themselves as "the good Christians." The *perfecti* (the perfect ones), as their opponents named them, that is, the "good men" and "good women," practiced absolute continence. The *perfecti* renounced marriage for themselves and administered their only "sacrament," the *consolamentum*. Sacraments, as such, they did not have, as material things are an essential element in every sacrament. The *consolamentum*, or rite of consolation, was administered by the laying on of hands of the *perfecti* and was given only once, often therefore delayed until one was close to death. The

---

10. See Malcolm Lambert, *The Cathars* (Oxford, UK: Blackwell Publishers, 1998).

consolamentum would save and protect one for the heavenly life from which one's soul had previously fallen into this material world. It was one's "baptism" into full membership in the Cathar Church, after which there could be no sexual relations or ownership of property. They practiced voluntary poverty and were generous at the same time. Ordinary believers, the *credentes*, accepted the teachings of the Cathar Church even if they had not yet submitted their lives to its disciplines, which was necessary once they had received the *consolamentum*. Among the *perfecti*, there were many convents of women as well as itinerant preachers.

Dominic could hardly have been prepared for such a world view—Christians denying the goodness of creation, the bodily incarnation of Jesus, marriage and the sacraments, the tradition handed down from the apostles. This encounter led him to articulate even more clearly than ever what he considered to be the truth in the Catholic faith—God, creation, incarnation, redemption, sacraments. What this all meant is retained in a story of Dominic in dispute with an innkeeper in Toulouse. He and the bishop and the retinue accompanying the bishop had taken a route through southern France. Staying in Toulouse at an inn, Dominic encountered its innkeeper, who was a Cathar. The story tells how Dominic stayed up all night disputing with the man. It manifests Dominic's passion for truth, for the truth of the gospel, and his call to hand on the fruits of his own contemplation. Would this dispute, or discussion, which lasted all night, the only night they stayed in Toulouse before moving on, have been considered preaching? The line would be thin between what took place in the pulpit in Osma to the choir and what was now needed in a new world for Dominic outside the choir. All the resources of his earlier life would have to come into play. Jordan has given us the account and said that the innkeeper "was unable to withstand the wisdom and Spirit which was addressing him" (*Libellus*, no. 15). Dominic brought him back to the faith.

Do we not at times find the same in our own lives? Everything that has gone before, from hindsight, looks like a preparation for a new challenge that was to come. Or is it just that everything we have done has provided a building block for what we must still do? Certainly it was this way for Dominic. His life of personal holiness, his love of study, his sensitivity to the poor, his university education, his contemplative and liturgical life as a priest, his deep faith in what the Church taught, his celebration of the Eucharist, preaching he had heard and had given, all this would now come into play as he met the challenge of a lifetime. For the Cathars were not just one innkeeper, but the journey to the north must go on. The bishop's business must come first. And so the wedding was arranged; the girl gave her consent. The trek back home to Osma included a wiser and more experienced man. Undoubtedly, Diego and Dominic, in their long journeys north, had talked about the Albigensians many times, as well as they would have with others in the bishop's party. But they arrived safely back in their beloved Castile, and Dominic was at home once again in his contemplative life as a canon, although still busy as the subprior. By now it would probably have been early in 1204.

THE KING, THE POPE, AND CISTERCIANS

Upon their return, however, King Alfonso, who was pleased with the results of the mission, engaged the bishop for yet another journey to be made not long thereafter to the same region up north, this time to fetch the bride. So in 1205, Diego, Dominic, and the bishop's retinue set out again. And once again, they would become increasingly aware of the heresy that was so widespread in the south of present-day France. The results of this journey would prove disappointing for the king but providential for the mission to which the Holy Spirit was calling Dominic and Diego. The young girl, for whatever reason, was no longer available. Jordan of Saxony suggests that she had died (*Libellus*, no. 16). Dominic's biographer M. H. Vicaire, however, had reason to suggest that the girl's father, in the meantime, may have allowed her to enter religious life, which would have created a complication for both the local bishop and the pope, since, in one sense, the girl at the time was considered legitimately married, having given her consent to marry the Spanish prince.[11]

It is certain, however, that Diego and Dominic began their return trip back home without good news for the king, and it is clear that they decided to return home via Rome. The reason may have been to submit the matter of this marriage to Pope Innocent III,[12] or it may have been to pursue with the pope Diego's desire to resign his episcopal see so that he could devote himself to a mission of evangelization, whether among the northern countries or amid Saracens or among the Cumans (a nomadic and barbaric people unknown to us today),[13] since he and Dominic had both become aware of the urgent need for proclaiming the gospel in those regions. Pope Innocent, however, still aware of the delicate balance back in Spain following the reconquest of territories there

---

11. Vicaire, *St. Dominic*, 53–55. Tugwell considers this question in *AFP* 68 (1998): 42–47.

12. See John C. Moore, *Pope Innocent III (1160/61–1216), to Root Up and to Plant* (Leiden: Brill, 2003).

13. Tugwell writes, *AFP* 68 (1998): 57, "We have no grounds for denying that it was Cumans, as Jordan says, not any northern pagans, for whose sake Diego wanted to resign his see in 1206." Also see pp. 48, 63, 72, and *Libellus*, no. 17. We do not know for sure who the Cumans were, but they are generally considered to be barbarians on the outskirts of Europe, whether on the southeastern edge, or some group that Diego and Dominic encountered in their second journey to the north, but at least a seemingly barbaric tribe. In Dominican history, they have come to symbolize Dominic's desire to preach among the unevangelized.

and thus of the need for evangelization at home as well as in far-flung territories, refused Diego's request to resign.

Pope Innocent III

Lotario dei Conti di Segni, a cardinal-deacon but not yet a priest, was elected pope on January 8, 1198, at the age of thirty-seven. He championed the freedom of the Church from lay or secular control—that is, the control of nobles, princes, and kings, over whom he attempted with great difficulty to maintain supremacy. An influential and reform-minded pope, perhaps the most powerful man in Europe at the time, he undertook the Fourth Crusade with the intention of recapturing the Holy Land. The results were disastrous. In 1204, the crusaders took and destroyed Constantinople against Innocent's wishes and plans. Nor did he later intend the extended destruction wreaked by the crusade against the Albigensians. Innocent summoned the Fourth Lateran Council in 1215, at which his concerns were the reform of the Church and the recovery of the Holy Land.

For reasons unknown, Bishop Diego took a route home to Osma through Burgundy with a stop and visit at Cîteaux.[14] At some point, Diego and Dominic would have become aware of a Cistercian mission among the Albigensians that had been entrusted to them by the pope, a mission of evangelization and preaching. They may well have heard of it from Pope Innocent himself. In the previous century, popes had relied heavily upon the Cistercians in varied ways. We will soon find Diego and

---

14. Tugwell, AFP 68 (1998): 57–60.

Dominic preaching along with these Cistercians. Preaching as a means of evangelization and conversion among the Albigensians and in the region of Toulouse had for some time now been part of Innocent's strategic plan. Of course, preaching was in the air, so to speak. There were varied preaching movements, some heretical, others suspect and on the fringe of the Church, as well as new religious foundations, not always easily delineated as to what was what. One can mention the Canons Regular, the Premonstratensians, and Robert d'Arbrissel,[15] all of whom contributed to the uplifting of the Church, as well as the Waldensians, who had been condemned in 1184.[16]

The Premonstratensians

The Premonstratensians, or Norbertines, the Order of Canons Regular of Prémontré, were founded in 1120 by St. Norbert (ca. 1080–1134), a friend of St. Bernard of Clairvaux (1090–1153). As canons, they followed the Rule of St. Augustine but added other legislation grounding themselves even more deeply in the common life, while they also exercised ministries of preaching and pastoral work. They were a part of twelfth-century reform efforts within the Church. At the time of Dominic, there was a Premonstratensian monastery near Osma with which Dominic would have undoubtedly been familiar.

---

15. Robert d'Arbrissel (ca. 1045–1116) was an ascetic itinerant preacher who lived a life of a hermit but founded many abbeys and communities of canons.

16. See Herbert Grundmann, *Religious Movements in the Middle Ages* (Notre Dame, IN: University of Notre Dame Press, 1995).

The Waldensians

Peter Valdes (or Waldes) from Lyons was inspired around 1170 to follow Christ as an itinerant and mendicant preacher. After providing for his wife and children, whom he left behind, he organized his own followers into the Poor of Lyons. Committed to lay preaching, voluntary poverty, and a strict approach to the Bible, they preached against the worldliness of the clergy as well as against the Cathars. Although he had the pope's approval for his life of voluntary poverty, Valdes and his followers were nevertheless not permitted to preach without an invitation from the local clergy, a prohibition they gradually ceased to honor. A central issue in their relationship to the Church was who had the right to preach. By 1184, they had been excommunicated and became organized outside the Church, questioning the validity of sacraments administered by unworthy clergy as well as the practices of venerating saints and relics. Nevertheless, the movement continued to spread and there remain small Waldensian groups even today.

In 1203, two Cistercians, Peter of Castlenau and Raoul of Fontfroide, had been sent to the Languedoc, authorized by Innocent III, on a mission of preaching and conversion. With them were their servants and retinue as well. The next year, the pope sent a third, Arnaud Amaury, Abbot of Cîteaux. The following year, 1205, Fulk of Marseilles, a former troubadour and a Cistercian, was elected bishop of Toulouse. In spring of the next year, 1206, Dominic and Bishop Diego providentially met with these three papal legates in Montpellier, where they commended the Cistercian commitment to the preaching but challenged their methods. Peter of Castelnau was the oldest of the three Cistercian legates. He would later be assassinated due to his strong opposition to the Count of Toulouse, who vacillated repeatedly with respect to his support of the Church against the Cathars.

These Cistercians were a distinguished preaching band in the heart of Cathar country. Success did not match their efforts, however. The pope, as concerned as he was, and as given to the idea of combatting the heresy through preaching, had instructed Diego to return home and had not allowed him to resign in order to take up an evangelizing mission elsewhere. His diocese would need him; he had already been away a long time. It would not be so much out of the way, however, and certainly not in defiance of the pope's interests, who probably had communicated to Diego and Dominic word of the Cistercian mission, to travel back to Castile via Montpellier, where the Cistercian preaching team had gathered. At least their return from Cîteaux back to Spain took them to Montpellier. Checking in with the Cistercian preachers was both wise and a delight. The pope had described the Cistercian mission as "consecrating oneself to the ministry of the word and of doctrinal teaching,"[17] which aptly describes the mission that Dominic and Diego themselves were desirous of undertaking.

Somewhere along the line, they had decided to see if they might not do something more. The problem as they now saw it, however, was bigger than they might at first have thought. Arnaud, Peter, and Raoul acknowledged that they did not have much to show for their two-and-a-half-years' worth of work. The challenge had probably been on Diego's and Dominic's minds for weeks. They could not count on the local clergy, who lacked

---

17. Vicaire, *St. Dominic*, 86.

education in doctrine and were not prepared as spiritual leaders but were basically administrators of the sacraments. The unreformed life of the local clergy was also one of the major obstacles to the success of the preaching. The legates of Rome themselves, however, were not exemplary in witnessing to the life of evangelical poverty, as they pursued their mission on horseback and with servants. The Cathars were formidable opponents. Unlike much of the Catholic clergy, who had become accustomed to a more comfortable life, Cathars lived simply, evangelically, and of their full members, one would say austerely. There was reason why the Cathars had forged such deep roots into the soil of southern France. Their way of life spoke volumes to simple people whose thirst for salvation was ever on their tongues. Diego and Dominic could see that, if they were to convey the truth of the Catholic faith, their primary witness to that faith would have to be in their way of life, following the example of the apostolic witness, the *vita apostolica* of the New Testament.

Dominic and Diego had had much time to ponder the situation. Whether the idea came from Diego or from Dominic we will never know; some ideas emerge from within a conversation and truly belong to neither one. But from what they knew, and it was confirmed when they arrived in Montpellier, the lack of success in the Cistercian preaching mission had less to do with the message than with the style, or one might say the way of life of the preacher. The abbot, as the bishop, had been accompanied by a retinue of men, traveled on horseback, and did not seem to witness to the evangelical poverty as well as much else in the gospels' portrayal of the life of Jesus. In that sense, the Cathar *perfecti* were more like Christ than the Catholic clergy or the Cistercian preachers. And so the idea—the birth, one might say—of the Dominican idea, is that they should preach the truth of the Catholic faith but live more like the heretics, more like the gospel—in other words, to live what they preached as the ordination rite even today requires of its priests.[18] One would not think it so novel an idea, but indeed it was. Both Dominic and Diego were willing to give it a try. The stopover on their way home had just taken a little more time, and now experimenting with this insight would prolong that a little more. Diego dismissed his retinue, and he and Dominic set out on foot to proclaim the good news. Peter and Raoul were willing to give it a try also. Arnaud had to return to preside over a general chapter. Diego was acknowledged as the leader for the team. They were all now mendicants, and they entered, whether nervously or fearlessly, major Cathar strongholds across the southwest of France.

---

18. In the Rite of Ordination of Priests, the bishop in these or similar words instructs those to be ordained: "Meditating on the law of the Lord, see that you believe what you read, that you teach what you believe, and that you practice what you teach."

CHAPTER 3

FORMATION FOR MISSION, 1206–1215

We do not know how successful these new preachers were. They certainly would have been perceived as different from other Catholic clergy. There were converts, of course, some at least, and many of these were women. Diego and Dominic began preaching in the area of Fanjeaux in southwestern France. Fanjeaux was a hotbed of heresy. Montréal, about five miles away, was also a Cathar stronghold. It was in Montréal, in the spring of 1207, that the "trial by fire" is considered to have taken place. Another tradition places it at Fanjeaux. It was not a one-day affair, but rather a disputation between Cathars and Catholics that lasted a couple of weeks. In order for this particular dispute to be resolved and the truth to be made manifest, Dominic placed the arguments, or at least New Testament texts, from the Catholic side in writing. Upon doing so, some Cathars decided to throw the sheet of paper into the fire to put its teaching to the test. If it burned, Dominic's argument was false. If it did not burn, the argument held and likewise the truth of the Catholic faith. The would-be judges, who were sympathetic to the Cathars, threw the paper into the fire three times, but it never burned, each time blowing back out of the fire. The story was reported by both Jordan and by Peter of Vaux-de-Cernai,[1] the latter placing it in Montréal, an authority followed by Vicaire in this case.[2]

In 1207, Diego and Dominic played leading roles in that debate in Montréal. Peter of Castelnau and Raoul, as papal legates, were also there, which testifies to the significance of the event. Shortly thereafter, twelve other Cistercian abbots arrived with some of their monks, who seem to have been assigned their own territories. Raoul died in July of that year. Diego, and possibly Dominic, participated in August or September in another formal debate at Pamiers, this one with Waldensians. The Cistercians continued their preaching under the leadership of Guy of Vaux-de-Cernai. Those associated with Diego continued as well. When Diego was not present, Dominic was in charge of Diego's team. Not long after the debate in Pamiers, Diego made a journey back to his diocese in Spain.

PROUILHE AND FANJEAUX

As "the Preaching"—or "the Holy Preaching" (as a later letter of Innocent seems to have referred to it[3])—continued, the

---

1. Among early sources for Dominican history, we have already mentioned the earliest of them, Jordan of Saxony's *Libellus*. After Dominic's canonization, there appeared later works by Peter Ferrandi, Constantine of Orvieto, and Gerald de Frachet's *Vitae Fratrum*. In the late thirteenth century came works by Stephen of Salanhac and Bernard Gui. Guy of Vaux-de-Cernai was a Cistercian abbot who later became the bishop of Carcassonne. His nephew, Peter, also a Cistercian, was the author of an *Histoire Albigeoise*, written from 1212–18.

2. Vicaire, *St. Dominic*, 104–05. Tugwell, *AFP* 73 (2003): 70–73.

3. Letter of March 10, 1208. See Vicaire, 107; 109–10; 472n78; 473n111. The name *Holy Preaching* came to designate Diego's and Dominic's "headquarters" for "the Preaching," centered in Prouilhe, referring to the entire project and mission. The expression had already been used by Gregory the Great but was applied by Inncocent III to the preaching mission among the Cathars. The term is already used in some of the early legal deeds of gifts given to the new community. It was not the community as such, but the preaching mission that was holy; this mission included not only "the preaching," but also "its way of life."

preachers separated to go to various centers, but Dominic and Diego remained in the area of Fanjeaux and Prouilhe, which are within easy walking distance of each other. They maintained temporary headquarters there. William Claret, a priest from Pamiers and a Cistercian monk, had joined them as well. Diego, however, had a problem on his hands. What to do with the women converts? Women had held a significant role among the Cathars, as they did in the history of religious life at that time.[4] The women could not return to Cathar homes or convents. Diego and Dominic had to provide for them in some fashion. They had to provide something comparable to the austerity of the Cathar life that the women were leaving behind. Some form of conventual life was necessary.

In December 1206, Diego and Dominic secured for the women an acreage where they could live the life of religious women, alongside the church of Saint Mary of Prouilhe. William Claret assisted Dominic in the material administration of Prouilhe. Juridically speaking, the women at Prouilhe were not nuns. It was not yet a monastery. The area became enclosed by 1211 but not confined even then to the women alone; there were laymen and -women living in the enclosed space. The first monastic buildings were not completed until 1211. Several of the women still had to live in Fanjeaux. Prouilhe was Dominic's first establishment. Or was it Diego's? Or was it both of theirs? Eventually it became a monastery, at first somewhat along Cistercian lines, since as of yet there was no Dominican rule. Later, after the Order was founded, it became Dominican.

There is a legend about the choice of the site of Prouilhe. One evening, Dominic was looking over the plain that stretched

---

4. One estimate is that 69 percent of the Albigensian *perfecti* were women. See Jonathan Riley-Smith, *The Crusades: A History*, 3rd Edition (London: Bloomsbury, 2014), 190.

in front of him from Fanjeaux and a globe of fire came to stand over Prouilhe. This happened on three evenings in a row. This *seignadou*—sign of God—was the sign he needed. God had spoken. This was the place and this is where he now belonged. *Alea iacta est*: "The die is cast." What Caleruega had been to his earliest formation, and Palencia to his education, and Osma to his vocation, Fanjeaux, Prouilhe, and Toulouse became in his continuing formation for mission.

We should give these women some note, as for the most part, their names are not so well remembered in history. Thus we pause here to call them to mind for their courage and faith: Raimonde Claret, Alazaïs, Richarde de Barbaira, Guilhelmine de Fanjeaux, Guilhelmine de Belpech, another Raimonde, Passerine, Bérengère, Jourdaine, Curtolane, Gentiane, and Ermessende—at least in so far as archives record.[5] These twelve, the majority probably being converts from Catharism, are some of the first to inhabit the new home in Prouilhe, down the hill from Fanjeaux. Prouilhe would shortly become something of a "double monastery," since it became a home for the preaching friars as well, coming and going as they necessarily would have to do. Yet the "monastic community" had their own prioress. Even when Dominic was more or less entrusted with its administration, he never as such became its prior.[6]

The year 1206 would go down in the annals of Dominic's life, as would 1207. Dominic and Diego continued their innovative approach to preaching. Eventually, however, the bishop would have to return home to attend to the needs of his diocese,

---

5. Vicaire, *St. Dominic*, 121–22, 477n74.
6. For much of the research into the beginnings of the house at Prouilhe and its history, we are indebted to Sister Barbara Beaumont, OP, of the Association of Sister Historians of the Order of Preachers in Fanjeaux. Also see Tugwell, "For Whom was Prouille founded?" *AFP* 74 (2004): 5–66, esp. 59–66.

which he did in September of 1207, intending also to secure funds for the preaching and the communities in Prouilhe, leaving his trusted companion and preacher behind to continue the preaching. Dominic was now on his own, although not alone, and undoubtedly missed his friend Diego, who had every intention of returning once he had attended to business back in Spain. But Diego was never to return. He died shortly thereafter, on December 30, 1207. When did Dominic hear the news? What was the grief that he bore, and what did it mean for him? Did he stay on? Could he stay on? It is what Diego had wanted. Dominic's life would now be the preaching: Caleruega, family, Palencia, student life, Osma, contemplative canon, and now Languedoc, the preaching. His years of initial formation had come to a close and it causes us to pause and ask what he and we may have learned entering the first months of 1208, when Dominic hears the news of Diego's death and also news of Peter of Castelnau's assassination. Diego's death, along with that of Raoul's, and then Peter's murder, all had dire consequences for the future of the preaching campaign.

Events unfold rapidly. By December 1207, Diego had returned to his diocese in Spain, entrusting the mission in the Languedoc to Dominic and William Claret. On January 14, 1208, Peter of Castelnau, who had remained with the preaching mission, was assassinated, ultimately putting Count Raymond of Toulouse under suspicion as being implicated in it. Count Raymond VI, the secular ruler, vacillated in his commitment to help uproot the heresy. He was intermittently excommunicated, forgiven, and then again excommunicated and forgiven. The pope was in an awkward position. It was his own commissioned representative who had been killed. He would canonize Peter, but what more needed to be done? The preaching had initially been his strategy, but it was evidently not as successful as he had hoped. Things had gotten no better. A new strategy was needed, but one that certainly cut to the core of Dominic. Pope Innocent declared war.

Raymond VI of Toulouse

Raymond VI was the powerful Count of Toulouse from 1194 to 1222. He vacillated between support of the Catholic Church and support of the Cathars, who were deeply embedded in his territories. Raymond was judged to be implicated in the assassination of the papal legate Peter of Castlenau, who had publicly excommunicated him in 1207 as a protector of heretics. He was also excommunicated (and pardoned) multiple times by Pope Innocent III: in 1208, in 1209, and again in 1211, after which he was not again reconciled until 1214. In 1215, Raymond went to Rome during the meeting of the Lateran Council in order to attempt to secure the territories he had lost. In 1217, he was able to retake Toulouse and defend it from Simon de Montfort, who died the next year in the siege. Raymond died while excommunicated and was denied a Catholic burial.

He called a crusade, a strategy that had been used by Innocent and other popes before. Many today find the word distasteful, but we have to put it in its medieval context.[7] It was a "holy war" that Innocent proclaimed against the Albigensians and secular rulers who may have been lax in their support of the Church, even dallying with the heresy themselves. Where the preaching seemed

---

7. For a brief, informative, and readable work, see John Vidmar, OP, *101 Questions & Answers on the Crusades and the Inquisition* (New York: Paulist Press, 2013).

inadequate, the crusade might succeed, or so Innocent thought—his intentions were noble. One of his own legates had been murdered. The pope called on Philip II (Philip Augustus) of France, whose motives in response included political ambitions. Philip did not participate in the crusade himself but encouraged his vassals and knights to do so and thus prepare for an expansion of France southward as well.

THE CRUSADE

Peter of Castlenau was canonized on March 10, less than two months after his assassination. On that same day, Pope Innocent called for the crusade, but it took time for men to be convinced and an army formed. Many crusaders signed up for only forty days at a time. Arnaud Amaury, the Abbot of Cîteaux from 1201 to 1212, the third of the papal legates, was appointed in March of 1208 to accompany the crusade and attend to its spiritual needs. The military mission was eventually entrusted to Simon de Montfort IV, who accepted it under some pressure from Abbot Arnaud. This put Simon in charge of the French forces on behalf of King Philip. He was from one of the aristocratic dynasties of northern France, a military genius, an exceptionally devout Catholic, yet ruthless. Simon de Montfort and Dominic would develop a good relationship, but the pope's decision to call for a crusade left Dominic in something of a quandary. Dominic is known during these years to have agonized about the fate of sinners in general as well as the heretics. He is reported to have prayed in a loud voice, "Lord, have mercy on your people, what will become of sinners?"[8] His prayer now must have been not

---

8. Tugwell, AFP 68 (1998): 39.

only, "What will become of sinners?" but also "What would become of the preaching?" Dominic did not lose his trust in the preaching. He would go on. Whatever he thought of the crusade, we will never know for sure. There is no evidence that he ever preached it, and he certainly did not participate in it.[9] He committed himself to preaching in the midst of it. His were dangerous times. This joyful man's life was to be one mixed with sadness.

Simon de Montfort

Simon de Montfort IV (ca. 1175–1218) was a nobleman from northern France who participated in the fourth crusade but refused to continue with it once it was clear that it was taking a turn unapproved by Pope Innocent III. He joined the Albigensian crusade in 1209 and, after the fall of Carcassonne, became its chosen leader. A devout Catholic opposed to heresy, he was also known for his ruthlessness in executing the war against the Albigensians. The religious motivation for the crusade was important for Pope Innocent. For de Montfort, there was also a strong motivation to increase the extent of his lands and wealth. Simon supported Dominic's efforts against the heresy, although Dominic was most probably not in southern France during the initial phases of the crusade. In 1213, Simon defeated Peter II of Aragon, Count Raymond VI of Toulouse's brother-in-law, in the battle of Muret, which seriously weakened the Albigensians, although Simon continued the war for his own gain. After a nine-month siege of Toulouse, Simon was killed on June 25, 1218. At first buried in the Cathedral of Saint-Nazaire in Carcassonne, his body was later moved, although a tombstone there still commemorates him.

On July 22, 1209, the Feast of Mary Magdalene, after the *Te Deum* had been sung, the massacre at Béziers took place. Fifteen thousand were reported to have been slaughtered in three hours. Women and children were not spared. Not even the Catholic population escaped.[10] By mid-August of that same year, partly due to fear of another Béziers, Carcassonne surrendered to the crusaders after two weeks. After that, Fanjeaux, Montréal, Mirepoix, Limoux, Pamiers, Castres, Lombers, and Albi all surrendered as well. It was in that same month that Simon de Montfort IV was chosen to lead the crusade and thus became the viscount of Béziers and Carcassonne, a title that was previously held by Raymond Roger of Trencavel, whose lands now belonged to Simon. Simon made his headquarters at Fanjeaux, in the vacant castle of a Cathar lord that had been deserted by the time he arrived. Simon also became a benefactor of Dominic, who may have baptized one of Simon's daughters[11] and did bless the marriage of Simon's eldest son, Amaury, in Carcassonne in June 1214.

---

9. On Dominic's noncollaboration with the crusade, see Vicaire, *St. Dominic*, 147, 151, 203. Vicaire writes, "Not a single document justifies us in thinking that Dominic collaborated in the crusade in any of these ways. Many of them, on the other hand, clearly establish that if he felt himself to be linked closely with the crusaders, he was not prepared to be their collaborator but kept himself apart" (147). If, as we will see Tugwell suggesting, that Dominic returned to Osma after the death of Diego until 1211, Dominic would not have been in the region during the first years of the crusade.

10. Aubrey Burl, *God's Heretics, the Albigensian Crusade* (Gloucestershire, UK: Sutton Publishing Limited, 2002), 39–45. Joseph Strayer, *The Albigensian Crusade* (Ann Arbor: The University of Michigan Press, 1971), 62–63, writes, "It is not true that the leaders of the Crusade shouted: 'Kill them all; God will know his own!' But the German monk who invented this story a few years later accurately reported the mood of the crusading army. In reporting the victory to the pope, the legate Arnaud Amaury said cheerfully that neither age nor sex was spared and that about twenty thousand people were killed. The figure is certainly too high; the striking point is that the legate expressed no regret about the massacre, not even a word of condolence for the clergy of the cathedral who were killed in front of their own altar." See also Vicaire, *St. Dominic*, 138, and John Vidmar, OP, *101 Questions & Answers on the Crusades and the Inquisition* (Mahwah, NJ: Paulist Press, 2013), 63 and 105n13, on the number slaughtered.

11. It is commonly held that Dominic baptized Petronilla at Fanjeaux in 1211, but the evidence is inconclusive. See Tugwell, *AFP* 73 (2003): 55–61.

Their relationship was not one of close friendship but neither was it distant. For Simon, war was war, and he had been familiar with crusades, having participated in the disastrous Fourth Crusade that Innocent III had called in hopes of retaking the Holy Land. One does what one judges one has to do to accomplish a task, as regrettable and shortsighted and tragic as that may be. The crusade against the Albigensians has been characterized as the most brutal religious war in history.

The campaigns in Languedoc under the command of Simon, and thus virtually the crusade itself, are more or less Simon's story. He took command in 1209 and became the viscount or ruler of Béziers and Carcassonne after their collapse. He failed to take Toulouse during attacks in 1211–12. Simon's fortunes waxed and waned: he was later victorious at the famous Battle of Muret in 1213,[12] in which Peter of Aragon, who had come to Count Raymond of Toulouse's assistance, was killed. Failing to take Toulouse, however, Simon returned again in 1217. In the course of that siege, on June 25, 1218, he was killed. In 1223, Louis VIII of France (whose wife was Blanche of Castile) became king. In 1226, he took charge of the crusade, won a decisive battle at Avignon, and died later that same year. The crusade itself only formally came to a close with the Treaty of Paris in 1229. The treaty provided for endowments for masters of theology and other masters to come and teach in Toulouse; these

---

12. This is the battle to which chroniclers a century later—such as Bernard Gui, OP (1261–1331), in an interpolation he arbitrarily made into Peter of Vaux-de-Cernai's *Histoire Albigeoise*—attributed the presence of St. Dominic, although there is no evidence to support this claim; in fact, the evidence suggests instead that it was simply an invention. Later followers of Dominic, including Bernard Gui, who in his *Life of Saint Dominic* spoke of Dominic as the first inquisitor, claimed that he was involved in both the crusade and the Inquisition, but the latter claim, as well, is untrue. There is a crucifix at Saint-Sernin in Toulouse, in the treasury in the crypt, recovered from the convent in Toulouse that later became a convent of the Inquisition. A tradition has maintained that it belonged to St. Dominic; see Guy Bedouelle, OP, *Saint Dominic: The Grace of the Word* (San Francisco: Ignatius Press, 1987), 183–90.

masters eventually became the beginning of a university in Toulouse. Cathars lingered on, now underground. They were not considered definitely defeated until the fall of Montségur in 1244. Yet the height of the war against the Albigensians was the campaigns directed by the military genius of the Count de Montfort.

Dominic's life itself was at risk. On the hill above Prouilhe, as one heads toward Fanjeaux, pilgrims today can still visit an assassin's cross, reported to be the site where assassins were ready to take Dominic's life as well. His response was lacking in fear, even somewhat cheerful. Jordan of Saxony reports him to have said, "I am not worthy of the glory of martyrdom; I have not yet merited such a death" (*Libellus*, no. 34), and so his life was spared. Providence again. But what was Dominic doing, and what was the burden that he bore?

DOMINIC, 1209–1215

In the years 1209 through 1211, what became of Dominic?[13] Between the meeting in Montpellier in 1206, the death of Diego in 1207, and Innocent's calling for a crusade in 1208, we have been able to follow Dominic fairly well. But what can we say about the period from the death of Diego, during the war, up until 1215, when Dominic established a diocesan preaching institute in the Diocese of Toulouse? How do we fill in the blanks? Dominic's biographer Vicaire writes, "Between August 1207 and May 1211, no dated account of an event, no document in the archives, has preserved for us the detailed narrative of the saint's activity."[14] Following Jordan of Saxony, who wrote, "While the crusaders were in the land, brother Dominic continued to stay

---

13. For Tugwell's chronological summary of these years, see *AFP* 73 (2003): 104–9.
14. Vicaire, *St. Dominic*, 142. See 137–63.

there up to the time of the death of the Count de Montfort, constantly preaching the word of God" (*Libellus*, no. 34), Vicaire understands him to have remained in the region during these years. Did Dominic unostentatiously move around from town to town, preaching, trusting in the power of truth, holding debates, making some conversions, and fostering peace? Was he disappointed that a crusade had been launched? Did he get discouraged? Dominic never joined the crusade. He never followed the Church's move from "Holy Preaching" to "holy war." There is naturally the question of what to do with disappointment in order to avoid the road to cynicism, for it is not a question of *whether* we will be disappointed in life, but rather of *how* we address it. This challenge will be either the beginning or the end of a profound spiritual journey. It must have been for Dominic. But was Dominic continuously in the Languedoc at this time, as Vicaire maintained?

These are dates about which we can be more certain:

1211—There is documented evidence that Dominic was in Languedoc in June to witness the bishop of Cahors' homage to Simon de Montfort and that Dominic had been put in charge of Prouilhe, which was more and more becoming a monastery proper.

1212—There is evidence that Dominic was at Prouilhe in May and in September. In December, he was elected bishop of Béziers but refused it.

1213 and 1214—Dominic was residing with the cathedral Chapter of Saint-Nazaire at Carcassonne as spiritual vicar to the Cistercian bishop Guy of Vaux de Cernai, who had been appointed by de Montfort in

1211. In 1213, Dominic preached a Lenten cycle in the cathedral.

1214—The papal legate, Cardinal Peter of Benevento, gave Dominic an official position as head of the preaching and faculties to deal with issues concerned with heresy, or at least he empowered Bishop Fulk to give him such a position. Dominic is also attested as holding the benefice of Fanjeaux (as a source of income for "him" and "his"). During this time, Dominic seems to have functioned somewhat as the parish priest for the town. In Carcassonne, Dominic blessed the marriage of Amaury VI de Montfort to Beatrice, the daughter of the dauphin of Vienne. Dominic worked in Toulouse as servant of the preaching (*minister praedicationis*). Sometime between mid-1214 and mid-1215, Dominic was elected bishop of Couserans but again refused to accept. Dominic evidently was well respected in the area and well enough known. Vicaire records a report concerning Dominic's refusals to be bishop: "[Dominic] was resolved to flee by night, carrying nothing but his staff, rather than to accept the episcopate or any other ecclesiastical dignity."[15]

In 1215, the preaching, the *praedicatio*, continued to take more and more shape. We will return to this later.

What can we say of Dominic between the death of Diego and Dominic's documented presence in Languedoc in 1211, that time during the assassination of Peter of Castelnau and the calling of the crusade? Did he remain in southern France between

---

15. Ibid., 152.

1208 and 1211,[16] or did he return to Spain, possibly making inter-mittent trips back to Languedoc?[17] Diego himself had evidently not been continuously absent from his diocese between the for-mulation of the preaching experiment in Languedoc and his return to Castile at the time when he died, for he was present at royal councils in Castile during those years and thus must have come and gone.[18] Unquestionably, Diego had placed Dominic in charge of the Holy Preaching and of Prouilhe as far back as early 1207. But from where did Dominic's authority come once the bishop had died?

"If, as seems to be the case, Dominic was involved in the Languedoc mission entirely on the authority of Diego," Tugwell writes, "then he had no warrant to operate or even to remain in the region once Diego was dead."[19] Strictly speaking, until 1210/1211, when Diego's successor, Menendo, was finally con-firmed and consecrated, there was no bishop in Osma who could authorize Dominic to remain away from his lawful chapter, nor is there any evidence of a "papal directive ordering or permitting Dominic to continue or resume his work there, or of any man-date allowing a papal legate to recruit preachers for the Midi in Castilian dioceses. [Thus] there is a definite presumption that Dominic had no canonical right to be anywhere other than Osma between Diego's death and Menendo's confirmation."[20] It is therefore difficult to prove either Dominic's presence at Osma or his absence from there. Whether or not he returned to Osma in 1208 and remained there until the spring of 1211,[21]

---

16. See Vicaire's thesis.
17. This is Tugwell's belief; see *AFP* 73 (2003): 5–69, esp. 5–15 and 69.
18. For a listing of the royal councils attended by Diego, see ibid., 70.
19. Ibid., 12–13.
20. Ibid., 14–15.
21. See Tugwell's hypothesis.

historians now fairly well accept that he had returned to Osma. He would have returned to Fanjeaux/Prouilhe by 1211 and thus, in 1211, would have picked up again the preaching and the responsibility for Prouilhe.

If Dominic had spent the majority of his time between 1208 and 1211 in Osma, with possible trips back to Languedoc that would have allowed continued contact with the community in Prouilhe, he returned there more definitely once Osma had a new bishop. He then took up his responsibilities in Fanjeaux, spending time there and in Carcassonne and Toulouse. By 1214, others began to gather around him, not only William Claret, but new companions. There was another Dominic from Spain, a Noel who would succeed him at Prouilhe, and others (Stephen of Metz, Vitalis) living with Dominic in Fanjeaux. Back in Osma, his heart must have remained with the mission in Provence and the Languedoc.

Raymond VI, the count of Toulouse, was again excommunicated on February 6, 1211, at the Council of Montpellier, the decree confirmed by the pope on April 17, and Catholic services in the city could not be held due to interdict. Bishop Fulk left the city for four years. He did not return until February 4, 1215.[22] The following April, Dominic founded a diocesan order of preachers. Dominic didn't give up. War was still ravaging the countryside, and Dominic continued and expanded his mission of preaching. In March 1212, Arnaud Amaury became archbishop of Narbonne. Dominic had not joined the crusade, nor had he acquiesced to being made a bishop. Dominic seems to have refused at least two, perhaps three, bishoprics—Béziers, Couserans, and Comminges.[23]

---

22. Aubrey Burl, *God's Heretics*, 89, 92, 142.
23. Tugwell, *AFP* 66 (1996): 64–66; *AFP* 73 (2003): 61–69. Vicaire, *St. Dominic*, 152, expresses doubt about Comminges.

Dominic's life itself had been threatened, yet he remained committed to a mendicant, itinerant, evangelical life, in a countryside ravaged by war, hatred, and greed. The crusade collapsed, more or less, by 1224. By then, Dominic was dead.

CHAPTER 4

FOUNDING A NEW FAMILY, 1215–1221

———ᘒᘓᘒ———

If Dominic returned to Osma following the death of Bishop Diego and did not return more permanently to the region of the Albigensians until 1211, he would have been back for four years as the preaching became focused in Toulouse. Upon his return to this region, Dominic had been attentive to the community in Prouilhe and had established himself in Fanjeaux. In 1215, however, Bishop Fulk and Dominic transferred the headquarters for the preaching to Toulouse and the bishop entrusted the preaching to Dominic and his companions. We now turn to the events of these next years.

1215

On February 6, 1211, Count Raymond of Toulouse had been excommunicated, and in late May, the city of Toulouse had been placed under interdict. Clergy and religious had to vacate the city. Dominic's focus had thus been Prouilhe, Fanjeaux, and Carcassonne, as we have seen. But on April 25, 1214, Raymond was reconciled with the Church. After a three-year absence, clergy were once again able to return to Toulouse along with their bishop, which opened the door for Bishop Fulk to invite Dominic to focus his energy on preaching from there. By mid-1215, Simon de Montfort had also established himself in the city of Toulouse.

Fulk provided Dominic with a facility dependent on the chapter of St. Etienne and the abbey of St. Sernin. There were new converts from among the women and close associates now from among the men. In April of 1215, two men of Toulouse offered themselves to Dominic along the lines of religious profession. Jordan reports it thus:

> At the time when the bishops were beginning to go to Rome for the Lateran Council, two upright and suitable men from Toulouse gave themselves to Christ's servant, Dominic. One of them was Peter Seilhan, who was later the prior of Limoges, the other was brother Thomas, a very attractive and eloquent man. Brother Peter made over to brother Dominic and his companions some tall, noble houses which he possessed in Toulouse near the Châteaux Narbonne, and it was in these houses that the brethren now first began to live in Toulouse, and from that time onwards all those who were with brother Dominic began to humble themselves more and more profoundly and to adopt the manner of religious. (*Libellus*, no. 38)

Peter Seilhan and his brother Bernard had inherited property, and on April 25, 1215, they divided it between themselves. Peter turned his share over to Brother Dominic, and thus a "religious house" was established in Toulouse. One can still visit the site today.

With the upcoming Lateran Council on the horizon, and with the crusaders along with Simon de Montfort now ensconced in the city, the papal legate, Peter of Benevento, to whom Dominic would have been officially accountable, returned to Rome. The preaching was now officially under the jurisdiction of Bishop Fulk, who assigned it to Dominic and his companions:

> In the name of our Lord Jesus Christ, We bring to the knowledge of all, both present and to come, that we, Fulk, by the grace of God humble minister of the see of Toulouse, in order to root out the corruption of heresy, to drive out vice, to teach the creed and inculcate in all sound morals, institute as preachers in our diocese Brother Dominic and his companions, whose regular purpose is to comport themselves as religious, traveling on foot, and to preach the Gospel word of truth in evangelical poverty.[1]

In this same decree, Fulk also provided for some of the temporal needs of the new community, which had become a preaching institute in his diocese. As Fulk refers to himself as the humble minister of the see of Toulouse, we find Dominic referring to himself as the *praedicationis humilis minister* (the humble minister of the preaching). Peter Seilhan's house provided the place. The Count de Montfort and Bishop Fulk provided for other needs. The brothers themselves already considered themselves bound by evangelical poverty—that is, living on alms as mendicants. Not yet having a church of their own, however, they were not able to have Mass in their house and were obliged to go to other churches in town. Often, this was the chapel of St. Romain not far away, which was given them the following year. By mid-1215, Dominic received another brother, William

---

1. See Vicaire, *Saint Dominic and His Times*, for this text, 171.

Raymond. In August, John of Navarre (also known as John of Spain) received the habit.[2] There was also the profession of the other Dominic from Spain, so there were now in Toulouse at least a minimum of six, possibly more. Still others remained in Prouilhe: William Claret, Brother Noel, and Brother Vitalis, whom we have mentioned previously.[3] As a witness to the value that Dominic placed on study, these first friars in Toulouse began to attend the lectures of Alexander Stavensby, an Englishman and professor of theology with the chapter of St. Etienne.

With the donation of Peter Seilhan's property, the self-offering of Peter and Brother Thomas to St. Dominic along with other companions, and the formal recognition of the preaching for the Diocese of Toulouse, Dominic was now set to accompany the bishop on his way to the Lateran Council in order that the two of them might visit with Pope Innocent III to report on the status of the preaching and to secure its future even further.

The Lateran Council

Innocent III convoked the fourth Lateran Council, the twelfth general council in the history of the Church, on April 19, 1213, to be opened on November 1, 1215. The council comprised over 400 bishops, about 800 abbots or superiors of monastic communities, and representatives of many of the kings of

---

2. On the early habit of the friars, see William A. Hinnebusch, *The History of the Dominican Order*, vol. 1 (Staten Island, NY: Alba House, 1966), 339–43. The habit, not unlike that of canons regular, comprised a white tunic, leather belt, a white scapular and capuce that was one piece, as well as a black mantle or cappa. The rosary was added in the sixteenth century. According to Jordan of Saxony (*Libellus*, no. 57), Reginald of Orléans was shown the habit of the Order by Our Blessed Mother in a vision.

3. The names of the early companions of Dominic can become confusing as sometimes they may be known by more than one name (John of Navarre, John of Spain) or dependent on a translation (John of Spain, Juan de España). I have maintained consistency throughout in how I refer to them, although I left to prudential judgment whether to translate a name or retain a more familiar version.

Europe. Among its seventy canons, the reform of the clergy, both bishops and priests, was a high priority, and made the council second in importance only to Trent as a reforming council. Innocent probably considered the council his crowning achievement. Clerics living sinful lives were to be suspended. Sees were not to be left vacant beyond three months; a chapter was to elect within that time frame or lose its right to do so. Bishops were instructed that it was their duty to preach or to arrange for assistance in this task. They were to assume responsibility for the education of clergy with a lector in theology in every cathedral. Laws were passed against clerical avarice and the misuse of relics. Everyone was obliged to confess their sins once a year and to receive Holy Communion once a year during the Easter season.

The council also established procedures for dealing with heresy. Several canons dealt with bishops' concerns regarding religious orders. The establishment of new orders, therefore, was forbidden, or at least an existing approved rule was necessary in order to do so. The council also dealt with the Count of Montfort's claims to the territories belonging to the Count of Toulouse. In this latter matter, Pope Innocent sought a mediated balance between those bishops supporting Montfort—who was as much interested in his personal gains as in the suppression of heresy, and into whose hands the legates of the pope had been drawn—and those supporting the Count of Toulouse. One can see in the work of the council several items that would affect the vision of Dominic.

In September 1215, Bishop Fulk, accompanied by Dominic, set out for Rome, with Dominic looking forward to a visit with Pope Innocent in order to set the preaching on a firm foundation. The pope himself had been invested in the preaching and had initiated it as far back as 1203, with the Cistercian mission among the Albigensians. While almost ten years had elapsed since Dominic's first visit, which took place after he and Bishop Diego returned from their second journey up north, Pope Innocent would remember that visit, as did Dominic. The preaching had originally been the pope's idea.

Dominic and Fulk both met with Innocent in October, before the meeting of the council itself, in order to seek papal confirmation of the preaching that had been established in the Diocese of Toulouse. This confirmation would make the preaching institute of Dominic and his companions more secure when the day arrived that Fulk would no longer be bishop there. With the council on the horizon and the concerns of bishops about the proliferation of religious orders, Pope Innocent wisely refrained from any quick decision with respect to Dominic's and Fulk's request. He turned it over to a cardinal respected in matters such as these, probably Cardinal Ugolino. Innocent and Fulk would turn their attention to the important work of the council, which held their sessions on November 11, 20, and 30.

We are now aware of the importance, although it is sometimes exaggerated, of the council's thirteenth canon. "To prevent the excessive variety of religious societies introducing a serious state of confusion into the Church, we formally forbid anyone soever from founding a new religious society in the future. Anyone who wants to enter religion must give himself to one of the approved orders. Similarly, anyone who in the future wants to found a religious house must take the rule and constitutions of some approved religious society."[4]

In December, following upon the council's concluding its work, Pope Innocent again communicated with Dominic. He naturally had to counsel Dominic in accord with what the council

---

4. Vicaire, *Saint Dominic and His Times*, 198.

had decided. Dominic would have to choose an existing rule if he wanted to go forward with his plans. But the question remains: What was Dominic's plan? What was his dream? What was he seeking from Pope Innocent? Did he come with Fulk to consult Pope Innocent because he wanted approval for a new religious order that he wanted to be called an Order of Preachers (*Ordo Praedicatorum*), as Jordan of Saxony suggests (*Libellus*, no. 40)? Setting aside for the moment whether the precise name of Order of Preachers (*Ordo Praedicatorum)* is something that Dominic was seeking, was Dominic actually asking Innocent to approve a new religious order at all? Or did he simply want confirmation of the shape that the preaching was taking in Toulouse—a religious institute in one way, but not a new religious order as such?

Vicaire, following Jordan's implications, concludes that Dominic was asking to establish a new religious foundation that would be an order of preachers and would have that name. Tugwell suggests that the name itself was not what was most important for Dominic. Even more noteworthy, however, it may have actually been Pope Innocent who initiated the challenge to Dominic to establish a new order that would be pontifical and not only diocesan in scope. Thus, when Dominic returned to visit the pope again in December, it was not simply that Dominic was gratified by the full support of the pope but that he was challenged to do more than he had asked for. Pope Innocent was the one who asked him to think big, beyond Toulouse, and thus he would have to choose a rule in order to fulfill the requirements of the council. Dominic went home, not saddened that he had not yet received final approval, but gladdened that it was clearly forthcoming. He was, however, even more so challenged by the prospect that now lay before him. It was most probably at this time that Dominic had the vision of Saints Peter and Paul to which Constantine of Orvieto refers: "The first, Peter, gave him the staff; Paul, the book; and both added—'Go and preach; for God hath chosen thee for this ministry.'"[5]

We have been accustomed to saying that Dominic established a community of nuns at Prouilhe, but it now seems more accurate to say that both Diego and Dominic did so, and whose idea it ultimately was, even if such could be pinpointed, will always remain obscure. Credit must certainly include Diego, as he was in charge. Their decisions would have been a collaborative venture. So once again Fulk, Dominic, and Innocent all collaborated in what propelled Dominic onto the world scene. What Dominic and Fulk came to present to the pope was transformed in the process. What they had wanted for a local diocese, Innocent saw as having greater potential. This was not Innocent's first encounter with Dominic. He would have perceived in Dominic strengths and gifts beyond what Dominic himself may have seen. And Innocent—in spite of the crusade—had still not given up on preaching. So from where did the idea come for a supradiocesan preaching program? Dominic had not come to ask for an *ordo praedicationis* in the sense of a new religious order, but it would seem that Innocent could see in Dominic and Fulk's request just such a possibility.

Two factors enter in. First, since this was not what Dominic had foreseen, what would such a burden place upon him? Second, the council itself would now have an impact on such a large venture. Given the burgeoning of so many new religious movements and communities, the council had decided that new ones ought not to be approved. Only traditional and already approved rules for religious communities were acceptable. Some parameters had

---

5. Ibid., 230. Tugwell, *AFP* 65 (1995): 31.

to be set. The question was how to get around this seeming obstacle. Dominic and his friars would have to adopt an already approved rule. None was more fitting, more flexible, for the mission at hand than the Rule of St. Augustine, with which Dominic would have been more than acquainted back in Osma. For Dominic, this was not his decision alone. He would need to return and consult the others. Dominic's style of leadership was always consultative. This is why it is difficult at times to separate Dominic from Diego, or from Fulk, or from the pope. No one decision was simply Dominic's alone, as later he would not want his order to be *his*. It was to be an order of Preachers. Its governance would be capitular.

What a shock the broadened scope of the preaching venture must have been for Dominic. He accompanied Fulk to Rome to ask support for a diocesan preaching mission and was being asked to inaugurate one for the whole Church. Did Dominic leave Rome, perplexed, perhaps shaken, feeling a new burden? It was not that Dominic was saddened by needing to wait for ultimate approval concerning a rule due to the legislation of the Lateran Council (for indeed that hurdle seemed fairly easily soluble). But he was being entrusted with the forming of a universal religious community from the small band of followers he currently had. On his journey back to Prouilhe, where he undoubtedly stopped on his way back to Toulouse, he must have wondered and pondered whether he had the gifts for this. If at any time Dominic's faith in providence was put to the test, it would have been then.

Dominic Returns Home:
What Had He Sought? What Must He Do?

Thus, Dominic returned to Toulouse to tell the brethren that he and Fulk had received Innocent's support. They could see the pope's suggestion as wise: Solidify and expand. Make it a legitimate religious community. As Tugwell writes, "It was not a crisis that Innocent provoked: it was an adventure. The little band of preachers trying to embody Diego's ideals in the Midi was challenged to become a world wide religious Order of Preaching."[6] Nevertheless, Dominic's mission, having become significantly widened, was also more complicated. He had left for Rome thinking that he already had a preaching institute that only required the pope's confirmation to become a stable *ordo praedicationis*. But now he had to start anew. If 1215 witnessed the first professions to Dominic in Toulouse as well as Dominic's and Fulk's trip to Rome, 1216 would pose new challenges and further decisions.

Did Dominic have his heart set on the new foundation in Toulouse being *called* an Order of Preachers? Tugwell maintains that the evidence does not support this, even if one's reading of Jordan gives this impression (*Libellus*, no. 40). Neither Dominic nor Fulk particularly espoused the precise term *ordo praedicatorum*, but rather spoke simply of a *praedicatio* (the preaching). Dominic himself spoke of himself as the *praedicationis humilis minister* (humble servant of the preaching). Fulk spoke of an *ordo praedicationis*. Both Dominic and Fulk later spoke of a *magister praedicationis*. When Dominic and Fulk met with Pope Innocent in 1215, they probably had the phrase *ordo praedicationis* in mind, with the sense of a stable institution but not as a religious order.[7]

What was the real impact of 1215 on Dominic? Yes, he was gratified by the commitments of Peter and Thomas Seilhan as well as by the support of Bishop Fulk. But even more so, following upon the visits with Pope Innocent, as Tugwell puts it, "The universalization of the *ordo praedicationis* which Innocent was proposing was something far bigger than what Fulk and Dominic had been asking for. How could the little band of preachers in Toulouse possibly match up to such a grandiose project?"[8] However we piece together the evidence, in January 1216, Dominic and Fulk were on their return journey back to Toulouse with work to be done.

1216

If 1215 had been both a challenging and a rewarding year for Dominic, 1216 would be climactic as well. In 1215, Dominic relocated the focus of his preaching from Fanjeaux/Prouilhe to Toulouse, received a quasi-religious profession from several brother-preachers, and was given a house in which they could live. He was acknowledged officially by Bishop Fulk as a preacher for the diocese and accompanied the bishop to Rome, where they had the opportunity to visit Pope Innocent. The pope encouraged him to think beyond the Diocese of Toulouse and found an order whose mission would be preaching, and thus to choose a rule for a new foundation in accord with the recent decisions of the Lateran Council. Dominic's head must have been ablaze upon his return trip to Toulouse via Prouihle, where he would have shared the new vision with his brethren. In May 1216, the brothers gathered to make a determination about which rule they would follow. It is unclear whether the gathering would have been in Toulouse or Prouilhe. A rule was also drawn up for the nuns in Prouilhe. In July, Bishop Fulk turned over the chapel of St. Romain in Toulouse for the preachers' use. They then had a

---

8. Ibid., 32.

church of their own, which more firmly and formally established them in the diocese. A cloister and cells were constructed to house them, and they were able to move from the smaller quarters they had had in the house of Peter Seilhan. All was going well when on July 16, Pope Innocent III, Dominic's supporter and collaborator, died.

Let us return for a moment to Count Raymond of Toulouse, a man not easy to pin down, and to the Count de Montfort. One could describe Count Raymond as "political" with the negative connotations of that term, a man willing to straddle the fence and see what was expedient. Sometimes Catholic, sometimes Cathar-friendly, his real allegiance was not easy to know. It has been alleged but not provable that he was responsible for the assassination of Peter of Castelnau. He may have expressed the desire, but it is difficult to trace the deed. The fact that he took a Cathar stance, or walked the tightrope, indicates that the Cathars were a formidable force in Toulouse. Toulouse, like Fanjeaux, was a Cathar stronghold. The heresy had sunk in deep roots. Innocent had hesitated to excommunicate Raymond but was under pressure to do so, and he did so more than once, with Raymond always relenting. It is thus that Bishop Fulk's diocese had come under interdict, with sacraments not administered and the Catholic faith not preached. But that changed as well. Although the Lateran Council had wanted to deprive Raymond of all his property, the pope preserved the title to some of it for his son and rightful heir. Since the council, the Count of Montfort was reigning in Toulouse and thus the mission of the preachers protected. On March 7, 1216, de Montfort forced the homage of the population in Toulouse, who had never been friends of the crusaders. Dominic, although friendly with de Montfort, did not owe his established presence there to him.

He could be grateful to Bishop Fulk and Peter Seilhan for that. Although the Order of Preachers celebrates 1216 as its founding date, the first friar to place his hands in the hands of Dominic and make profession did so in 1215—Peter Seilhan, in Peter's home in Toulouse, which he later bequeathed to Dominic.

Dominic and his brethren made a decision, and Dominic needed to let them know what might lie ahead, although Dominic himself may not have known with any clarity. Was this a moment of fear or of joy for them? What would this mean? For now, they would still function in the diocese of Toulouse. But the dreamers among them—and by now Dominic himself would have been one of them—saw their work in a new light. Jane's dream was becoming true: this friar's bark would be heard throughout the world. Of course, at this point, they had no sense that they themselves would be moving from the region in which they felt so at home. They would not necessarily have dreamed of being sent far away. But first things first: they selected a rule for themselves, fulfilling the requirement of the council for a new order, but still needed final approval from the pope, although they were assured of his support. They had easily concurred that their rule would be that of St. Augustine.

Dominic knew that his heart's desire required another trip to Rome to seek Pope Innocent's authoritative approval. There was no reason to think this would be denied—except that Pope Innocent III died on July 16. The brethren had chosen to follow the Rule of St. Augustine. It readily fit their way of life. It was the rule with which Dominic had been familiar in Osma. They supplemented it with other legislation as well, *consuetudines*, influenced by the customs of Prémontré.[9] But then there came a new pope.

---

9. See Vicaire, *Saint Dominic and His Times*, 206–12. Also see Simon Tugwell, "The Early Dominican Constitutions," in *Early Dominicans*, 455–70, who shows how the early constitutions both borrowed and modified the legislation of the Premonstratensians.

Dominic and Pope Honorius III

As difficult as they may have been to predict, Dominic's meetings with Pope Honorius went well. Dominic needed to bring Honorius up to speed and provide certain assurances.

Pope Honorius III

Cencio Savelli was a native of Rome, loved by the Romans, and one who had distributed much of his own possessions to the poor. He had been a member of Innocent III's college of cardinals and was committed to Innocent's agenda. He was elected to succeed Pope Innocent on July 18, 1216, two days after Innocent had died, and served until 1227. Like his predecessor, he played a significant role in the politics of Europe and shared his goals of the recovery of the Holy Land and the reform of the church. In 1216, with the bull *Religiosam vitam*, he approved Dominic's Order. He approved the Franciscans in 1223 and the Carmelites in 1226. In 1220, he crowned Frederick II Holy Roman Emperor.

Honorius was the pope with whom Dominic would deal for the rest of his life. He would find the pope to be as helpful as was Innocent. Honorius provided a number of letters or papal documents in support of the preaching and the Order. In the end, Honorius deserves the credit for giving Dominic's new order the authoritative stamp of the Holy See, making it an order of pontifical right, which would be so necessary in the years ahead when it met and would continue to meet grave opposition, from bishops, monks, and secular clergy. Critics would wonder how this new venture could be called "Religious Life." They were not monks. There was no monastery and therefore no stability. These had been replaced by a so-called itinerancy. Give no heed to the fact that Jesus had no place to lay his head. These mendicants seemed to mooch off the people for their livelihood and considered begging to be something respectable. They appeared to be more like wandering beggars. They had the approbation of the pope, however. Honorius confirmed the venture, and the itinerant mendicants were given juridical status in 1216—the official date for the founding of the Order of Preachers.

The situation was more complicated than might appear on the surface. The necessary consistory of cardinals was held, and Cardinal Ugolino was among them. On December 22, 1216, Honorius III confirmed Dominic's new foundation. But the approval for its mission as that of preaching was not yet secured, pending further discussions between Dominic and Ugolino.

Cardinal Ugolino

After the death of Pope Honorius III in 1227, by which time Dominic had also died, Cardinal Ugolino, a nephew of Pope Innocent III, was elected and took the name of Gregory IX. As cardinal, he, too, had befriended Dominic, and may well have been the cardinal to whom Innocent sent Dominic in 1215 to explore his proposal further. Gregory IX formally instituted the papal or medieval inquisition. He canonized Francis of Assisi in 1228 and Dominic in 1234. In 1233, he established a university in Toulouse.

The approbation came from Honorius on January 21, 1217. The papal bull or document of 1216 confirming the Order was addressed to Dominic, prior of St. Romain of Toulouse, and to his brothers, present and to come.[10] The Order at that time was still conceived in official documents as an order of canons but with the right to expand. Dominic and his brothers were clearly now a religious order. In the wording of the 1216 text, however, there was no clear recognition, as such, of the mission of the Order as that of *praedicatio*. Dominic clearly had the support of the new pope, who collaborated with him, as had Pope Innocent. There were to be more than sixty supportive papal bulls or documents in the years before Dominic died. Much trust was placed in him. And on January 21, 1217, Honorius addressed one of these documents to the preachers (*praedicatoribus*). The identity and mission of preaching was acknowledged. In December 1216, Honorius III had given Dominic's diocesan order of preachers his seal of approval and confirmed them as an *ordo religiosa*. In January 1217, he confirmed preaching as the *raison d'être* of the Order. They were to be *praedicatores*.

It was thus Honorius who actually referred to the new foundation for the first time as an Order of Preachers, giving all the final approvals necessary. In a papal bull of 1218, Pope Honorius explicitly designated the Order as *Ordo Praedicatorum* (Order of Preachers). This seems to have been its first appearance in records. Although Jordan of Saxony gives the impression in his *Libellus* (no. 40) that Dominic had desired this title, it seems doubtful. Up to that point, Dominic and Fulk had only used *ordo praedicationis*. Tugwell comments, "Thanks to Honorius the project first dreamed of by Diego, first realized by Fulk, reshaped by Innocent and made viable by Dominic had won its place as *ordo*

---

10. Vicaire, *Saint Dominic and His Times*, 220, also 225, and 240ff. For a more detailed presentation of data pertinent to the varied papal documents issued between 1218 and Dominic's death, see appendix VI of Vicaire, *Saint Dominic and His Times*, 418–525. Ugolino clearly emerges as a strong support for St. Dominic as was Honorius III.

predicatorum in the universal church."[11] Although this may be a question of a distinction that makes no difference, for Dominic it had always been simply a question of the *praedicatio*—the preaching. For him it was always the preaching, not the preacher, who was never to get in the way of the Word.

1217

The Order had been confirmed on December 22, 1216, and its identity as an order of preachers acknowledged on January 21, 1217. Dominic left Rome around February and returned to Toulouse by March, when he gathered the brothers to share the good news. Before leaving Rome, he had a conversation with a William of Montferrat in which they dreamed about preaching together among pagans in the north. After his return to Toulouse during spring, he also shared his plans for dispersing the brethren. Later in the same year, he would make a return trip to Rome. What Osma had been for Dominic in his early formation, and Prouilhe, Fanjeaux, and Toulouse were for his later formation, Rome would now become. His life journey took him from Caleruega's rural countryside to Rome's ecclesial and urban life.

Unlike some events in Dominic's life that may seem more legendary than historically verifiable, his encounter with William of Montferrat while still in Rome in early 1217 is documented. No sooner had the Order been confirmed than Dominic's efforts at recruitment began. William had come to Rome for Lent and was staying with Cardinal Ugolino, which allowed Dominic to meet him. They soon became friends, which reflects once again Dominic's capacity for friendship, and

---

11. Tugwell, *AFP* 65 (1995): 45.

William decided to join the mission that Dominic was so enthusiastically embracing. He and Dominic talked about preaching together. Dominic's evangelical zeal surfaced amid all the business he was forced to undertake on behalf of the nascent Order he was founding. Both agreed that William needed further study and theology. So he would go to Paris for two years of study. Then they would meet and together evangelize in pagan regions farther north. It was not to happen, but a spiritual friendship was forged within a sense of a common mission. William would have been one of the first recruits following the confirmation of the Order.

The pact made with William indicates that Dominic did not see his vocation as a preacher being only among heretics but rather to unbelievers as well. It was a missionary spirit that moved him. It may have been at this time that Dominic allowed his beard to grow, although it is not certain when he actually decided to do so and for how long he may have had one.[12] Dominic seems to have been a missionary at heart, or perhaps a preacher at heart says it better. Dominic was with Bishop Diego when they first met with Pope Innocent in 1206 and Diego wanted to resign his see in order to evangelize among the mysterious Cumans.[13] That this was Dominic's desire as well is not difficult to surmise. While Dominic later spent much of his time in Cathar country, he was naturally drawn to preach against the heresy, because that was the context in which he found himself. But his desire had always been for the salvation of souls and not for any one group in particular. The enthusiasm that he and William now shared indicates again the broader scope of Dominic's vision and calling. As Tugwell writes,

---

12. Vicaire, *Saint Dominic and His Times*, 227, suggests that Dominic may have grown a beard at this time. Tugwell places it later, *AFP* 68 (1998): 68–70: "It is very probable, then, that Dominic was bearded at least during the first half of 1221, and it is quite likely that he was also bearded for a time in 1219."

13. See chapter 2.

"Dominic longed for the salvation of everyone and wished to devote himself utterly to that cause, even to the extent of martyrdom,"[14] and "Dominic's zeal for the salvation of unbelievers was obviously not restricted to any particular people."[15] Dominic, too, had his Cumans.

Dominic was dreaming in other directions as well and made use of his gifts for governance and strategic planning. How was the new Order to extend the preaching beyond the Languedoc? The brethren were well established in Prouilhe. The political situation in Toulouse, however, was becoming unstable. Simon de Montfort's foothold there was insecure. What would happen to the preaching if Toulouse once again succumbed to the control of Cathar sympathizers? It could be the end of what had just begun. Both Dominic's emerging vision of a worldwide mission and his apprehensions about the possible fate of Toulouse led him to the decision to disperse the brethren so that Toulouse would not be their only stronghold. He gathered the brethren together at St. Romain to announce his decision.

The Great Dispersal

More and more men had begun to join Dominic. Some had been laymen, while others were canons from Osma, and still others from other religious orders. In 1215, there had been William Claret, Noel, Vitalis, Peter Seilhan, Thomas of Toulouse, William Raymond, John of Navarre, and the other Dominic from Spain, all of whom have been previously mentioned. Now, in 1217, there came Matthew of France, previously from the chapter in Castres; other Castilians, among whom was Dominic's own

---

14. Tugwell, *AFP* 68 (1998): 40.
15. Ibid., 71. For Tugwell's discussion of Dominic's wider sense of evangelization beyond simply the antiheretical campaign in southern France, see *AFP* 68 (1998): 33–85; and vol. 66 (1996), 41–46, 76.

brother, Mamés, also Miguel de Ucero from near Osma, as well as Miguel de España, Pedro de Madrid, and Gómez. Other new ones included Lawrence from England; Odier, a lay brother from Normandy; and Bertrand of Garrigues from Toulouse itself, whose family later gave the Order the site of the future convent there when St. Romain became too small. Dominic himself finally broke his own official ties with the chapter of canons in Osma. All of these friars would be affected by Dominic's decision. The joy he brought with him upon his return from Rome was now mixed with sorrow about their impending separations and departures. Not all of the brethren were convinced or pleased, nor was the bishop. In which direction might disaster lie, in remaining together in Toulouse or in being dispersed? Dominic was convinced of the wisdom of the latter.

There are varied accounts of visions and suprasensory experiences that Dominic had, but one of the more trustworthy is that of a vision of the imminent death of Simon de Montfort. Jordan described it in the following way:

> In 1217 the people of Toulouse determined to revolt against Count de Montfort, an event which we reckon the man of God, Dominic, had foreseen in spirit some time in advance. He had seen a vision of a tall, beautiful tree, in whose branches a large number of birds were living. Then the tree was felled, and the birds which were sitting on it all took to flight. Filled with the Spirit of God, brother Dominic realized that the great and exalted prince, the Count de Montfort, patron of many people, was soon to meet his death. Invoking the Holy Spirit, brother Dominic called the brethren together and told them that he had decided to send them out, few as they were, into all the world;

he did not want them all to go on living there together for much longer. The announcement of this sudden dispersal amazed them, but their confidence in the evident authority which his sanctity gave him made them more prepared to agree to what he said, because they were hopeful that it would all lead to a satisfactory outcome. (*Libellus*, nos. 46–47)

Time was not on Dominic's side. If we set his year of birth as 1173, he would have been forty-four—young by our standards but not by that of the thirteenth century. The war was still going on. Dominic set about the task not only of preaching but of organization. The decision to disperse the men was both to protect the preaching and to expand it. The political situation in Toulouse was volatile. Dominic interpreted his dream as signifying the imminent death of Simon de Montfort, a military genius even if one who could be ruthless who had also been a benefactor for Dominic and whose organization of the crusade made Toulouse a Catholic city. (De Montfort was, in fact, killed about a year later, on December 13, 1218.) What would happen upon Simon's death? If Toulouse returned to Catharism, an interdict might be placed on the city. If so, what would become of the preaching? The only way to save the fledgling effort was to scatter the flock. An early chronicler recorded that "hoarded grain goes bad, but it fructifies if it is scattered."[16]

In August 1217, on the Feast of the Assumption according to some accounts, the actual moment for the dispersal had come. Whether this took place from Toulouse or Prouilhe is hard to determine. Where to send them would not be difficult—to the great cities of Europe and their universities. Paris would come

---

16. See Simon Tugwell, "Introduction," in *Early Dominicans*, 16.

first, then Madrid, eventually Bologna. They would be sent out as disciples of old had been sent—and not always with willing acceptance but resigned nevertheless. Dominic was, however, already manifesting his gift for governance and asked the brothers to elect a superior. Matthew of France was chosen. He was to be sent to Paris. He had the title of abbot, and until 1220, held the title in Paris of "Abbot of St. Romain," which carried with it more the connotation of prior. The title of abbot was used only this once in Dominican history.[17] Dominic was clearly the one to whom religious professions had been and would be made, but were something to happen to Dominic, the Order would go on.

Two groups were being dispersed to Paris, the theological center of Europe. A university had been well established there by the time it was formally chartered in 1200 by Innocent III, who had also studied there. It was the first of its kind. Its luminous reputation drew Dominic's attention as the place where the Order needed to be. The first group of brothers comprised Matthew of France, Bertrand of Garrigues, John of Navarre, and Lawrence from England. The second group comprised Dominic's blood brother Mamés, Miguel de España, and the lay brother, Odier. They departed on the same day, but the second group arrived first, on September 12. The first group arrived three weeks later. Four brothers were also sent to Dominic's native Spain—Pedro de Madrid, Gómez, the other Dominic from Spain, and Miguel de Ucero. Still others, natives of Toulouse, remained at the convent of St. Romain. Among them were Peter Seilhan, who would before long also go to Paris and later found a community in Limoges; Thomas from Toulouse; and possibly William Raymond, if he had not died or was no longer with them. There

---

17. On the significance of this title, see Tugwell, "The First and Last Abbot," in *AFP* (1999): 5–60.

is little record of him. Toulouse was thus not being abandoned. Noel as superior; William Claret as administrator; and possibly Vitalis, if he were still there, remained in Prouilhe.

Not all went smoothly. It is quite natural to feel the pain of ties that had bound the men together being torn asunder. They had formed a community. The preaching of the Brothers of St. Romain is that to which they had given themselves. Some saw wisdom in Dominic's decision, but not all. John of Navarre especially exemplifies the resistance. Unwilling to go in the first place, he was especially unwilling to go under the circumstances, that is, of mendicancy. For Dominic, this was never an option. The imposition of mendicancy, however, had only been imposed on the brothers by the charter in Toulouse. The document from Rome that had confirmed the Order had left the role of mendicancy in the expansion of the Order unclear. It was an emotional moment for Dominic. Would making an exception here set a precedent and justify a relaxation of the poverty that gave evangelical witness and substance to the preaching? Dominic relented, however, giving John twelve pence, feeling reassured by the other six going to Paris that this would not become custom. Having learned of insurrection in Toulouse, possibly cut off from the brothers at St. Romain, Dominic set out for Rome by mid-December after meeting with Bishop Fulk to settle affairs pertaining to the brethren in Toulouse.

1218

Dominic left for Rome by the middle of December 1217. The Order had been confirmed, the brothers' identity as *praedicatores* authorized, and the dispersal accomplished. Now further organizational work was needed. The brethren of St. Romain in

Toulouse had truly moved onto the worldwide stage. Dominic had to face this task as well as to carve out time for the preaching itself, his first love, his calling. The year 1218 saw a flurry of activity, even if we cannot always pin down where Dominic may have been at any one time.

In Rome, by sometime in January or February 1218, having traveled on foot and now even more zealous for the mendicant and itinerant life to which the preaching had called him, Dominic met again with Pope Honorius and received further letters of recommendation from the pope for the mission of the friars. One of these, dated February 11, 1218, was the first bull of commendation recommending to bishops "the friars of the order of preachers whose useful ministry and religious way of life we believe pleasing to God."[18] This was the first time that the expression *ordo praedicatorum* officially designated the Order. The Lateran Council had encouraged bishops to attend to their responsibility to preach, but in this commendation, they were instructed not only to preach themselves but to accept the preachers of the Order.

During this time in Rome, John of Navarre, who had been studying in Paris, and another friar with the name of Bertrand came to give a report from the Preachers in Paris. The other Dominic and Miguel de Ucero returned from Spain disheartened with their efforts there. These were all sent to Bologna to make a foundation. Bertrand and John may have been sent before the end of January and Miguel and the other Dominic toward the end of March or early April. When Dominic himself later left Rome and stopped by Bologna on his way to Spain, at least John of Navarre and the other Dominic seem to have accompanied him

---

18. "Fratres ordinis predicatorum, quorum utile ministerium et religionem credimus deo gratam," Tugwell, *AFP* 65 (1995): 41.

on that journey.[19] It was also in Bologna that two angels miraculously supplied the brothers there with bread in response to St. Dominic's prayer.

Dominic also received Reginald of Orléans into the Order who would also be sent to Bologna as Dominic's vicar there. Reginald had studied at the University of Paris, had taught canon law there for five years, and then had been appointed dean of the cathedral chapter in Orléans. During the course of a pilgrimage to the Holy Land, he stopped in Rome, where he met Dominic, whose way of life persuaded Reginald to enter the Order. Dominic's prayer brought about a cure for Reginald, who had fallen seriously ill. Our Blessed Mother, according to Jordan who had heard Dominic himself relate the story, appeared to Reginald, saying, "I anoint your feet with holy oil to make them ready to spread the gospel of peace" (*Libellus*, no. 57). Upon his return from the Holy Land, Reginald was to go to Bologna, the second great university center and home of the most significant canon law faculty. He arrived there on December 21, 1218. One of those whom Reginald himself attracted to the Order after he had later been sent to Paris was Jordan of Saxony. Reginald died in 1220, a year before Dominic himself. Dominic treasured him as one of his finest recruits.

Sometime in May, Dominic left Rome after having taken care of business there, and undertook what today we would call visitations. By the end of 1218, in accord with Dominic's dream, Simon de Montfort was killed in battle in Toulouse. It was a significant moment for the crusade, for Toulouse, and for the Order. Dominic was undoubtedly grateful for his decision to disperse the brethren. Although the details of this period are difficult to confirm, Vicaire suggests that Dominic visited Bologna on his way out

---

19. Tugwell, *AFP* 65 (1995): 53–80.

of Italy from Rome, and then made his way through Provence, stopping at Prouilhe. It was perhaps at this time that he also adapted the life of the women there more to the customs of the Preachers as those had evolved, and then continued to Toulouse, which, after late July, was no longer under siege and was thus safe. Yet it is difficult to verify the actual route that Dominic took; much is conjecture.[20]

Dominic's *terminus ad quem* on his departure from Rome was his native Spain along with the preaching and friars there. We do not know whether Dominic returned to Caleruega, Palencia, or Osma.[21] If he had been in Osma for the years following the death of Diego, there may have been no need to retrace those steps for nostalgia's sake now. What we do know is that Dominic established houses in Madrid and Segovia at that time. In Madrid, there would have been only a small group of the brothers. Dominic also gave the habit to several women who were entrusted to the friars, in contrast to the history of Prouihle, where the women were established first and to which a community of brothers became later attached. This was the origin of what would be the monastery of nuns in Madrid, to whom Dominic later wrote our only extant letter of his. The other Dominic from Spain who was a *socius* of Dominic on the journey

---

20. Tugwell does not see Dominic stopping by Prouilhe and Toulouse on the way. See Ibid., 57–58, 79–80, 82–86. Did Dominic, on his way from Rome to Bologna, stop by and visit a Franciscan general chapter? It remains a disputed question. Tugwell would suggest that, if Dominic ever visited a chapter of the Franciscans, it would more likely have been in 1216 on his trip to Rome to meet with Pope Honorius. See Ibid., 58–60, 80–82, 143. A Franciscan tradition has Dominic visiting a general chapter of the Franciscans in January of 1221. Vicaire, *Saint Dominic and His Times*, 344. Evidence for whether Dominic and Francis ever met, or when, is inconclusive. Also see Hinnebusch, *The History of the Dominican Order*, vol. 1, 154–55.

21. A convent in Palencia is considered to be the second house of the province of Spain, but there is no evidence to trace its founding as far back as 1218 or 1219. The earliest evidence seems to be for 1220, and so there is no evidence that Dominic visited there on this journey.

was placed in charge of the friars and the women. Later, in 1219, when Dominic arrived in Paris in the course of his 'visits,' he sent his brother Mamés from there to Madrid. The letter that Dominic wrote to his sisters in Madrid refers to Mamés as "our most dear brother."

Dominic's journeys involved not only attentiveness to the friars and the formalizing or establishing of a more regular life for the men as well as for newly recruited women, but also and especially a ministry of the Word. Dominic was first and foremost a *praedicator*, a Preacher. Thus it was also upon his arrival in Segovia in late December. Dominic preached not only in Latin but also in the vernacular.[22] There were new recruits, a house was donated, and a convent established, all giving witness to the power of Dominic's preaching. The house in Segovia came to be considered the first convent of Preachers to be established in Spain, as the house in Madrid before long became a monastery of nuns with only a few brethren attentive to them. Jordan described it very succinctly:

> In the same year [1218], Master Dominic went to Spain, where he founded two houses, one in Madrid, which is now a monastery of nuns, and one in Segovia, which was the first house of the friars in Spain. In 1219 he returned to Paris, where he found a community of about thirty friars. (*Libellus*, no. 59)

Taking the last sentence to heart, the friars were expanding faster than the impression we may have given; thus Dominic's visits were needed. Dominic was not the only one recruiting; the friars themselves did so upon their arrival in a new place. Even in Segovia there may have been some friars there before Dominic arrived.

---

22. Vicaire, *Saint Dominic and His Times*, 254.

1219

When Dominic actually departed Spain and left for Paris we cannot be sure. The first months of 1219 leave this datum unclear. In his journey, he passed again through the south of France and would have heard of increased trouble for the brethren in Toulouse as well as for the monastery and convent of friars in Prouilhe. They remained troubled times. This would be Dominic's last time to visit Toulouse. In late May or early June, Dominic left Toulouse for Paris in the company of Friar Bertrand, who was in Toulouse from Paris, and they arrived at the convent of St. Jacques, where thirty some young friars waited to meet and welcome Dominic. Matthew of France and the friars had done well with their recruitment. That Dominic had a gift and deep love for the contemplative life can be documented as far back as his days in Osma. That he was called to an itinerant life became more and more obvious after 1211 but certainly during the latter years of his life. In 1218, having attended to business in Rome, he was on the road preaching as well as making pastoral visits to the brethren: Madrid, Segovia, Toulouse, Paris, and Bologna. The preaching continued through 1219 and the years following.

Dominic had become an itinerant and mendicant contemplative, begging people for material sustenance and begging the Lord for spiritual nourishment, praying for God's mercy and that of his brothers. Dominic was both contemplative and itinerant. He not only integrated both but was able to be both simultaneously. This is the picture of his inner and outer life that emerges, a deep integration, a man of prayer with a mission, a contemplative missionary. His being "on the move" is why it is difficult to pin down accurately so many of the details of where he was during the latter years of his life. From Paris, he was on the road again to Bologna, and we cannot be sure of what stops he made along the way, what preaching may have happened, or his thoughts about possible new locations for evangelization and houses for the Holy Preaching. His dream—the dream that he shared with Diego and with Pope Innocent—continued to unfold as it was made more and more real in the two years that remained. Dominic was an evangelist, a midwife, an instrument in the hands of God. He had become a humble servant of the preaching. What portrait of St. Dominic, of St. Francis, did St. Ignatius have in mind when he would write in his autobiographical reflections four centuries later, "Suppose that I should do what St. Francis did, what St. Dominic did?"[23] If only he could be another Dominic, another Francis, Ignatius discerned. He too was called to contemplation in the midst of action.

Dominic would have reached Paris in June 1219. The convent of St. Jacques played a central role in the early history of the preaching friars. It was not only a community living the regular life but a *studium* or house of study. The convent itself was in the shadow of the University of Paris. In Paris, Dominic was able to connect again with Brother Matthew of France; with his own brother Mamés; with the others from the original group who had been dispersed approximately two years earlier; with Peter Seilhan, who was now there; and with the new brethren, such as the first German to join the Order, Henry of Marsburg. On one of the occasions when he was preaching, Dominic also met Jordan of Saxony, who confided in Dominic but was not yet ready to join. Reginald of Orléans would have the privilege of receiving Jordan and Jordan's friend Henry into the Order. Dominic was also at this time able to give the habit to William of Montferrat, whom he had met in Rome in 1217 and with whom he had talked about their future preaching together. William had

23. *St. Ignatius' Own Story, as Told to Luis Gonzales de Camara*, trans. William J. Young (Chicago: Loyola University Press, 1956/1980): 9–10.

now completed two further years of theological study and would accompany Dominic to Bologna. The extent to which mendicancy should be practiced remained a disputed question in Paris but was later resolved along lines of a stricter observance.

Wherever Dominic went, he met the friars with encouraging words, continued the practice of public preaching, and opened himself to the possibility of new foundations. In Paris, he chose once again to disperse some of them. There were after all about thirty gathered there. There had already been a foundation from Paris in Orléans. Dominic now sent Mamés to Madrid. Peter Seilhan would go to Limoges. Perhaps it was at this time that some were sent to Rheims. He may have also discussed with Matthew the possibility and desirability of Reginald's return to Paris, which Dominic could execute upon his arrival in Bologna. Dominic left Paris for Bologna by mid-July after having stayed there not much more than a month, but a profitable month it had been. William of Montferrat was one of the brethren to accompany Dominic, as he would later do so as well on trips to Viterbo and Rome.

In Bologna, Dominic and the friars traveling with him were welcomed as much as if not more than they had been in Paris. There was also a large community in Bologna as well as a convent in conjunction with the church of St. Nicholas of the Vines under the care of Reginald. Since his arrival on December 21, 1218, Reginald had helped the community in Bologna to flourish. His preaching led Jordan to describe him as a new Elijah who had risen among them (*Libellus*, no. 58). Dominic sent Reginald to Paris, where he accepted Jordan and his friend Henry into the Order. Later, upon being questioned by Matthew of France as to whether he had any regrets about submitting himself to the rigors of the life of the Preachers, Reginald replied, "I very much doubt if there is any merit in it for me because I have always found so much pleasure in the Order" (*Libellus*, no. 64). Reginald, undoubtedly to the joy of Friar Dominic, had been and was rigorous with respect to the practice of poverty.

Once the friars had been granted the church of St. Nicholas, they needed more land in order to construct the convent. The owner of the land, Pietro di Lovello, was not so eager to make a sale. His granddaughter, however, Diana d'Andalò, who had become a good friend of the Preachers after hearing Brother Reginald's preaching, succeeded in persuading her grandfather. He sold the land on March 14, 1219, and the friars were able to move in close to Easter. They were there by the time Dominic and his companions arrived in late August. Dominic was impressed with the resources: new friars among whom there were many eager students as well as some who were already masters in canon law; the university itself as second only to Paris; and an established convent. He chose to make Bologna his home, except for the times when he would need to be in Rome or preaching in nearby dioceses—still the itinerant, still the contemplative.

Not long after his arrival, Dominic had the pleasure of meeting Diana d'Andalò himself, who was greatly attracted to Dominic and his holiness. Before Reginald left for Paris, Diana made profession in Dominic's hands and vowed obedience, even though there was as yet no monastery or convent for women in Bologna. Her step, however, would be the beginning of the monastery of St. Agnes, which was not ready yet at the time of Dominic's death.[24]

---

24. Diana's formal connection to the Order began with her promise to Dominic in 1219. There having been a delay in the construction of a Dominican monastery for nuns in Bologna, Diana remained at home living a religious life. Then in 1220, she attempted to join a monastery of Augustinian nuns at Ronzano, but was forcibly removed from there by her family. Dominic was later able to meet with her in her family's presence when back in Bologna. The monastery dedicated to St. Agnes did not get established until after Dominic's death. In 1223, Diana, along with four others from the monastery of San Sisto in Rome, among whom was Cecilia, who was to be the prioress, entered the monastery within the octave of the Ascension.

Diana later became particularly close with Brother Jordan, and throughout the centuries, his letters to her have given a remarkable witness to their spiritual friendship.[25] What Dominic had done with Diego in Prouihe, and did later in Madrid, he envisioned for Bologna. Dominic's ministry to women who were called to a deepened spiritual life is worthy of note. Both at this time and later, a sizable number of women were moving into religious life, and a significant percentage of the Cathar *perfecti* were women as well. Not so long after Dominic's death, the Order had to face how much of its attention could be devoted to the pastoral care of its women. Dominic's own outreach was noteworthy, however, from the first establishment in Prouilhe to the work at San Sisto in the last year of his life. They were family for Dominic as much as were his friar preachers.

As he had done in Toulouse and Paris, Dominic sent brethren forth from Bologna as well. He sent some to preach in Bergamo, which would be the second community of friars in Italy, to Florence where there were preaching friars as of November, and probably at this time to Milan and Verona. He was envisioning sending brothers as far as Scandinavia. In the community in Bologna, there were already two Swedish friars. It was during this time that Dominic also sent Brother Reginald from Bologna to Paris, which was not good news either for the brethren at St. Nicholas or for many in the city. Vicaire writes, "The bonds were already too long-standing and too deep to be broken without suffering."[26] Jordan wrote the following:

> Brother Reginald, however, he sent off to Paris. His sons, whom he had so recently brought to birth by the word of the gospel were deeply distressed and wept to

---

25. Gerald Vann, *To Heaven with Diana* (New York: iUniverse, Inc., 2006).
26. Vicaire, *Saint Dominic and His Times*, 276.

be torn so soon from the loving breasts of their accustomed mother. But all these things were done by God's
will. It was one of the most remarkable things about
the servant of God, Master Dominic, that, when he
sent the brethren hither and thither throughout the
various parts of God's church, as has been mentioned
already, he always did so with complete confidence; he
never hesitated or wavered, even though other people
sometimes disagreed with what he was doing. It was as
if he knew exactly what was going to happen, or as if
he had been given instructions by the Spirit in some
revelation. And who would venture to say that it was
not indeed so? (*Libellus*, nos. 61–62)

Having accomplished much in Bologna, Dominic went
with William and others to Viterbo via Florence. There Pope
Honorius and the Roman curia had been meeting since October.
Dominic was in Viterbo by November 11 at the latest and had
two requests to make of Pope Honorius. First, he wanted letters
of recommendation that could be submitted to diocesan clergy
requiring that they receive and support the ministry of the
preaching friars because conflict between diocesan clergy and the
mendicants had begun to surface. Second, he wanted to request
that mendicancy would be officially incorporated into the
Order's legislation. Both were granted. The "bull of mendicancy"
was dated December 12. These were all sent to various houses of
the Order. Dominic would also have to attend to the question of
a possible house in Rome and deal with a complicated matter at
the request of the pope, that of San Sisto. By sometime in
December, Dominic made his way to Rome. But before proceeding to the complex matter of San Sisto, let us pull together a few
further thoughts pertinent to mendicancy and the Order, since

mendicancy and voluntary poverty were at the heart of Dominic's evangelical strategy.

Mendicancy and the Preaching Friars

The practice of voluntary poverty and mendicancy within Dominic's vision of the Holy Preaching manifested both continuity and evolution.[27] Evangelical poverty was part of Dominic and Diego's project from the beginning. Its importance for Dominic can be found in what has come to be considered his last will and testament before dying. Although not an accurate reporting of something Dominic actually said on his deathbed, it is an accurate reflection of his life: "Have charity, preserve humility, and possess voluntary poverty."[28] Yet how the practice of poverty was to be enfleshed developed between the days in Fanjeaux and those in Toulouse and between those in Toulouse and the upcoming general chapters of the Order to be held in Bologna, as the Order itself evolved and faced ever new challenges. As far back as 1206, the preaching was to be on foot, without money, seeking hospitality through begging for food and shelter. The begging was to be for one day at a time, although this was not a hard and fast rule. The Holy Preaching owned no property. It needed no property. They lived on alms, which for Dominic was not only an imitation of Christ and the apostles but also liberating, "to ensure that no worldly responsibilities and worries would hinder their job of preaching" (*Libellus*, no. 42).

With the donation of Peter Seilhan's house, however, and the organization of the Holy Preaching as a diocesan institution

---

27. For a more thorough discussion of the voluntary poverty movements of the thirteenth century as manifest among monks, hermits, canons, laymen, and friars as well as their social contexts in an increasingly urban society and the challenges thus presented, see Lester K. Little, *Religious Poverty and the Profit Economy in Medieval Europe* (London: Paul Elek Ltd., 1978).

28. See Tugwell, *Early Dominicans*, 59.

in Toulouse, Dominic was faced with a place where preachers would live, find supplies, be cared for if ill, or just rest while not on the road. For this, some form of revenue or endowment was necessary and would be of benefit to the preaching. The bishops could be counted on to help from resources available to them. Such was the case with Bishop Fulk in Toulouse, who assigned them one-sixth of the tithes from parish churches in his diocese. This too was a form of alms but only applied to the "convent" in Toulouse. When the brothers were itinerant, they still carried no money, begged, and depended on hospitality. Thus the preaching from Toulouse in 1215 had to face realities that Dominic and Diego had not had to face in 1206. They needed a home, and now they had one, whether Peter Seilhan's house or that of St. Romain. The more permanent center was quasi-endowed with funds from the bishop, but the preaching friars still practiced mendicancy. In addition, the need would shortly emerge to attend to the intellectual formation of new brothers once they had been dispersed. How far should mendicancy extend? Should it cover even conventual life once there were houses in Segovia, Paris, Bologna, and elsewhere? The itinerant mendicancy was never a question; conventual mendicancy was something new to be addressed.

The struggle over the application of the ideal of evangelical poverty and the practice of mendicancy would emerge anew with the dispersion of 1217, as witnessed in the reluctance of John of Navarre to travel to Paris with nothing and Dominic's response as a blend of hesitancy, sadness, and kindness in conceding to allow him twelve pence for the journey. The common practice, of course, even obligatory for canons, was that a superior was to provide for the expenses of someone's journey. Begging was not considered acceptable, a fact that contributed to the struggle mendicants would have in making their way of life credible. There was no legislation yet in the Order; indeed, there was hardly an Order yet. In Toulouse, they were living the life of canons regular according to the Rule of St. Augustine. Yet Dominic's vision was clear. Matthew of France and the brethren at St. Jacques in Paris would need to address and readdress the questions. They first lived in "abject poverty." Then through the generosity of donors, they were "endowed" in a fashion similar to that of St. Romain, which enabled the purchase of books, clothing, and other necessities along with care for the sick. Yet Matthew too had to give in at times, even allowing travel on horseback or occasionally the carrying of money. Dominic would have encountered this on his visit to Paris in 1219. It would have made him think: how widely can mendicancy be practiced? To what degree could his own personal ideal and practice be a sufficient basis for the emerging more stable foundation? In Paris, he had also found some opposition to his increasingly radicalized approach to poverty.

Dominic faced the same challenges when he came to Bologna, where he, in fact, refused a generous donation of property, although here Reginald was of a common heart and mind with Dominic on the question of poverty. There was still to be no property, only some form of endowment as revenue, living on alms. But with the upcoming chapter, mendicancy would be on the agenda. Pope Honorius's "bull of mendicancy" that Dominic had requested in the previous December made the practice legitimate for the friars but not obligatory with respect to many details. This is a decision the brethren themselves would have to make. The expression *mendicant poverty* had not yet come into use. The pope had spoken about preaching "in the lowliness of voluntary poverty."[29]

---

29. Latin *"in abiectione voluntarie paupertatis."* Vicaire, *Saint Dominic and His Times,* 283.

Back at St. Jacques, upon receiving from Dominic the words of the pope, they decided as a community to "abandon the care of our life for the present and for the future to the assistance of divine Providence."[30] As much as the question of evangelical poverty would have been on Dominic's mind at this time, so the request of Pope Honorius with respect to San Sisto would now occupy him.

San Sisto

Pope Honorius, who was one of Dominic's major human supports, faced another challenge for which he envisioned Dominic as a solution. Innocent III had already desired to establish a monastery in Rome comprising women from monasteries that were deteriorating or that had become lax in their observance. Honorius intended to pursue this project but thus far had been unsuccessful. Now it seemed as if the right person for the task was at hand. A church (known as San Sisto) dedicated to St. Sixtus II, a third-century pope and martyr, would be the site. Prouilhe could be the model and the sisters and brothers in Prouilhe and Fanjeaux could help. The pope saw this as first and foremost a convent for nuns but possibly also as a foundation for the friars as well. Such had been the reality in Prouilhe. By the end of 1219, Dominic and some companions had settled into the church with the need still to construct a convent. It would take much of Dominic's energy to convert the site into a monastery of stricter observance for nuns, to gather together women for that purpose, especially from Santa Maria del Tempulo, nuns with whom Dominic had previously become acquainted. Dominic had to leave Rome before being able to bring to completion the in-gathering of nuns at San Sisto. He would return to the task in 1221.

---

30. Ibid., 285.

1220

Toward the end of February 1220, Dominic wrote to his brothers in Spain, France, and Italy, as well as to more isolated brothers, instructing them to choose representatives to come to Bologna. On May 17, 1220, the Feast of Pentecost, there would be the first General Chapter of the Order of Preachers. At the same time, Dominic learned of Brother Reginald's death in Paris. Dominic's gift for leadership was more and more being made manifest. He continued with organizational tasks as well as with continued preaching. A bull dated February 17, 1220, acknowledged Dominic as *prior ordinis praedicatorum* or prior of the Order of Preachers. Up until that time, Dominic had held the Order together by his moral authority, by the affection of the brethren, and as the recognized founder. The new wording or title not only indicated the pope's confidence in Dominic but also gave his role a juridical basis or clarity. How the varied houses of the Order were to "hang together" and what their relationship one to the other might be were questions the upcoming Chapter would have to face.

The Chapter would be the ultimate governing instrument. It was a democratic form of governance, although not in our modern sense; it was perhaps more parliamentary, not new in religious history but adapted to meet the needs of the friars. It was not a gathering of all the friars. That had become impossible. Representatives were chosen from various houses or regions so that the whole Order would be represented and consulted. These brothers then came together to deliberate and legislate, to appoint and elect. Among those elected at the Chapters were the major governing superior—or provincial—of each province or region. Each province, in turn, would have several priories, and the superior of each priory (the prior) was elected by the members of that priory.[31]

By sometime in March, Dominic was back in Viterbo. He sent friars to Verona and Milan and saw to the establishment of a house in Palencia. His student days must have seemed long past, and yet the city was about to witness the emergence of a university similar to those that already existed in Paris and Bologna. On May 16, after a stop in Florence, Dominic arrived in Bologna for the Chapter. Many of the almost thirty delegates to the Chapter, having come from Madrid, Segovia, Provence, and Paris, had not seen each other during the previous three years. Among those from Paris was a recent recruit of Reginald's who had been professed only months earlier, Jordan of Saxony.

The story of Dominic's life at this point became the story of the Order and of Dominic as a founder. This is too often how we remember him. It must be told to make his life complete, but it is not the whole Dominic. The preaching movement had advanced beyond Dominic's earliest expectations, if he had expectations more than fear. Something organizationally now had to be done. Dominic wanted nothing more than to be a preacher, and a friar among his friars, but this task had been given to him and he took up the cross. The 1220 chapter of the whole Order was called in Bologna to begin to give shape and form to what the Spirit was doing. A chapter is an authoritative and representative fraternal gathering to do both legislative business and executive action. Eventually, one of its primary responsibilities would be to conduct elections and make appointments. The first task at hand in 1220 was the need for constitutions. The Rule of St. Augustine as an overarching guide, along with the "customs" (*consuetudines*)

---

31. Later general chapters would take up the task of further structuring. Simon Tugwell has done extensive research on "The Evolution of Dominican Structures of Government." See *AFP* 71 (2001): 5–159; vol. 72 (2002): 27–105; vol. 75 (2005): 29–79.

that had guided them since 1216, had served their purpose well up to this point but were insufficient for a growing international movement.

THE CHAPTER OF 1220

The primary objective of the gathering of representatives from the Order was to attend to the necessary organizational challenges that confronted the Order and, from Dominic's perspective, to consider his role in the ongoing formation of the Order. Undoubtedly conscious of his own diminishing health, Dominic wished to step aside, although his moral authority and the fraternal love with which he was held were stronger than ever. He is reported as having said to his brothers, "I deserve to be deposed for I am useless and lax."[32] Perhaps he meant "useless" in the sense of declining health and "lax" in the sense of having less energy than before; it was an expression of true humility on his part. His brothers refused the offer. They could not at this point envision the Order without Dominic as their head. He had brought the Holy Preaching to birth and was needed to continue its remarkable growth, but his request allowed them to elect him. His authority hereafter, as well as the authority of future Masters, did not come from papal approbation but from the election itself, from the chapter, from the brethren.[33]

Once this decision was made, Dominic introduced the structure of electing members, called diffinitors, who were charged

---

32. Vicaire, *Saint Dominic and His Times*, 302. See Tugwell, *AFP* 66 (1996): 103–6.

33. Tugwell writes, "It has come to be a jealously guarded privilege of the Order of Preachers that the election of its Master needs no confirmation by anybody, not even the Holy See," *AFP* 72 (2002): 27. For the development of this privilege, ibid., 27–105, esp. 74–79, 102–5. Also see vol. 66 (1996): 82–88, esp. 82n133, and 105, tracing this privilege back to Dominic's request that he be deposed and in turn being elected.

with overseeing the business of the Chapter.[34] While in session, the Chapter was the supreme vehicle for governance. It became a legislative body. Upon its completion, Dominic, or the Master, would function in an executive role. In this sense, there was already a division of powers. What the Chapter decided was no longer simply considered to be "customs" (*consuetudines*), but rather "institutions" (*institutiones*), which later came to be called "constitutions" (*constitutiones*). How binding were these constitutions legislated by the Chapter? Dominic's previous confidence in a principle of dispensation was now acknowledged by the capitulars. Statutes are binding, but a superior has the "power to dispense the brethren in his priory when it shall seem expedient to him, especially in those things which are seen to impede study, preaching, or the good of souls, since it is known that our Order was founded, from the beginning, especially for preaching and the salvation of souls."[35] In addition to the power of dispensation on the part of superiors, it was also decided that the legislation of the Order did not bind under pain of sin, in contrast to that inscribed in the Rule of St. Benedict. Thus, there existed in the Order the two primary instruments of governance: the general chapter, legislative in nature, and the head of the Order along with local superiors, executive in character. The pope continued to recognize Dominic as Prior of the Order (*prior ordinis*), but the brethren saw him as Master (*magister*), or Master of the Preaching (*magister praedicationis*), or Master of the Preachers (*magister praedicatorum*). Dominic remained the Master of the Order, but a system of capitular governance was set in motion. Chapters were to meet annually at the time of Pentecost, alternately in Bologna

---

34. Tugwell, *AFP* 66 (1996): 88, 106; vol. 71 (2001): 12–16.

35. In the Primitive Constitutions, dated to the Chapter of 1220. See *Saint Dominic, Biographical Documents*, ed. Francis C. Lehner (Washington, DC: The Thomist Press, 1964), 212. Also Vicaire, *Saint Dominic and His Times*, 304.

and Paris. The Chapter of 1221 would again be in Bologna, and that of 1222 would be in Paris. By that time, Dominic had died. While a Chapter was being held, it was the governing body and even the Master was under its jurisdiction.

In addition to these fundamental principles of organization, the Chapter of 1220 also dealt with the office of preaching, the practice of mendicancy, and studies. Brethren who are capable of preaching are to be presented to the chapter to receive the license to preach. They are to speak only with or about God. They are to be free from the concerns of temporal administration unless there is no one to take care of such matters. They shall not carry with them any money and begging for money was also excluded. One could beg for food, clothing, or books. They were to go out two by two; it was forbidden to travel alone or on horseback. Neither property nor revenues of any kind were to be accepted. The Chapter adopted the practice of both itinerant and conventual mendicancy. Study was also given significant attention; the position of master of students was created for this purpose. Only theology should be studied, neither the secular sciences nor philosophy. The preacher was to be an ongoing student of theology.[36] The Order was to be an order of students.[37] As Tugwell put it, "As early as 1220 the order was in principle committed to making every house a school with its own *doctor*."[38]

Following the Chapter, Dominic must have felt relief. The Order could now go on without him if God were to call him home. Preaching friar that he was at heart, he was now free to return to preaching and turn his attention away for the moment from the burden of administration. Yet, at the insistence of his

---

36. Further details are given in Vicaire, *Saint Dominic and His Times*, 308–14.
37. I found this felicitous expression in C. H. Lawrence, *The Friars, The Impact of the Mendicant Orders on Medieval Society* (London/New York: I. B. Tauris, 2013), 84.
38. *AFP* 71 (2001): 30.

brothers, he remained the Master of the Order of Preachers and that would continue to carry with it responsibilities. Following the close of the Chapter, during the latter part of 1220, he traveled throughout northern Italy where the Cathars were both strong and divided among themselves. In Lombardy alone, there were four different and opposing Cathar sects. There was a Cathar Church in Florence and they had even made inroads into the Papal States.

The medieval world of the thirteenth century in which Dominic found himself was a world in transition. An old order was beginning to pass away, and a new one was being born. The new form of religious life manifest among Dominic's itinerant, mendicant, preaching friars was designed to fit a new moment of history. Not only was evangelization a great need; new structures were needed for it to flourish. For over a century, there had been rapid economic changes, an increase in commerce and wealth, growth of population, and urbanization. With these had come a rise in lay literacy as manifest among the Humiliati, a more or less twelfth-century lay movement that eventually comprised monks and canons as well and became a recognized order of penitents known by their simple dress. This rise in lay literacy was often accompanied by religious dissent and anticlericalism—as among the Waldensians, for example—or by heresy, as we have seen among the Cathars. Monasteries were no longer the only centers of learning. With the rise of urban universities such as those at Paris, Bologna, and Oxford, there emerged a scholastic theology fueled by the newly translated works of Aristotle that rivaled the traditional monastic theology. The city and not only the desert had become the locus for a living out of the gospel and its apostolic way of life. This new evangelization would be a challenge, indeed.

Dominic preached in season and out of season, speaking only of God and with God, not only in the market place but also to the brethren, in Latin and in the vernacular, in Castilian but also in the varied dialects of northern Italy as he had previously done in the Languedoc. Witnesses attest to his preaching in German as well, whatever an occasion might require, calling people to conversion, hearing confessions, establishing new foundations, and performing miracles through the power of his prayer. In Lombardy, there were four convents: in Bologna, Bergamo, Milan, and Verona. In a city in which the Preachers were to be established, a church for their use was obtained from or offered by the bishop, but the diocese retained its ownership, since the friars themselves were still renouncing ownership of property and the convent maintained itself through the practice of mendicancy. Conventual mendicancy as well as itinerant mendicancy was practiced. We need not retrace in detail Dominic's footsteps to see that for the remainder of 1220, he continued as an apostle of Our Lord Jesus Christ. Before the end of the year, Dominic had gone back to Rome.

1221

By the end of December 1220, or at least by mid-January 1221, Dominic had arrived back in Rome, doing further business with the papal curia and pursuing further the establishment of the monastery of San Sisto. The brothers were fairly well established at San Sisto, but Dominic needed to attend to the relocation of nuns there. That could not be complete until nuns from Prouilhe would arrive to help, but there was much to do in the meantime. The challenge was to make it an observant monastery. The two principal monasteries in Rome that were to be brought together at San Sisto were those of Santa Maria in Tempulo and

Santa Bibiana. Part of Dominic's plan for the renewal of the religious life of these women included the practice of strict enclosure. Many of the nuns resisted because it had not been part of their previous practice, yet Dominic's preaching and spiritual guidance were persuasive. The nuns from Santa Maria in Tempulo would gather in the church of San Sisto and make profession in Dominic's hands, although it was not yet ready for them to move there.

The nuns, however, had placed a condition on their willingness to move, which they undoubtedly thought was in their favor. They possessed in their monastery an icon of the Blessed Mother that had refused to be housed elsewhere. On an earlier occasion, it had been taken by Pope Sergius III to the Lateran but had come back to Santa Maria "flying like a bird through a window." Thus, the sisters insisted that if the icon refused to move to San Sisto, they too could be exempted. When the actual time came for the relocation, a procession by night brought the icon, where evidently it was willing to remain, and thus the sisters too. In order for the sisters to be able to move, however, adequate housing had to be found for the majority of the brethren living there. For this, Dominic was able to secure from the pope Santa Sabina on the Aventine hill. Once they had relocated, so could the sisters. Five nuns came from Santa Maria, fewer than that from St. Bibiana, as well as eight from Prouilhe. They were given the tunic, scapular, and veil of the nuns of Prouilhe and Madrid. The nuns from Prouihle had been able to arrive in order to prepare the way for the relocation. The nuns entered the new monastery on February 28, the First Sunday of Lent.[39] Dominic appointed Sister Blanche from Prouilhe the prioress and provided

---

39. The nuns remained there until 1575 when they moved to where the Angelicum in Rome now stands. In 1931, the monastery and icon were transferred to Monte Mario outside Rome.

them with a rule and constitutions. Several friars were left there as chaplains as well. The long struggle to bring together the nuns into the enclosure at San Sisto and to establish a community of the brothers at Santa Sabina brought to a close the work that he needed to do in Rome. Santa Sabina would eventually become the headquarters for the Order. Dominic left Rome for the last time shortly after May 10, 1221, to return to Bologna and another Chapter of the Order.

Santa Sabina

The Basilica and Priory of Santa Sabina on the Aventine hill in Rome remain to this day the headquarters of the Order of Preachers. St. Sabina had been a second-century martyr. In the fifth century (422–32), a basilica was built in her honor by Peter of Illyria, which also came to house her relics. It became one of the principal titular churches in Rome under Pope Gregory the Great. It is the oldest extant basilica in Rome to preserve its original plan. For centuries, it was the custom of the pope to come to Santa Sabina to bless and distribute ashes on Ash Wednesday. The custom was discontinued in the eighteenth century but revived again in 1960 by Pope John XXIII. In 1221, Pope Honorius III gave the church to St. Dominic after four friars previously residing at San Sisto needed to move. Even today, one can visit "St. Dominic's cell," which originally was the section of the dormitory nearest the basilica where Dominic sometimes slept and from which he could quietly leave to pray in the church.

Dominic's attentiveness to the San Sisto project manifested not only his gratitude to the pope for all that he had done for the

Order but also Dominic's own respect and appreciation for women religious. They had been his first converts in Prouilhe for whom he and Diego had established a convent. Then there were women converts in Toulouse. The monastery in Madrid was the next to be founded once friars were established there as well. His vision had often involved the establishment of a monastery for women along with that of a house for the Preachers. Unfortunately, the only extant letter of his that we have is that to the nuns in Madrid, written in 1220, although he wrote extensively to his brothers as well, for which we have evidence even if not the letters themselves. In Bologna, he had received the promise of profession on the part of Diana; however, due to the circumstances beyond his control, the monastery of St. Agnes in Bologna only came to be in 1223 after Dominic had died. San Sisto was just another manifestation of his keen intuition of the role that women were to play in his Dominican family.

The Rule of San Sisto is the earliest rule for Dominican nuns that we have, and the earliest text for it dates from 1232.[40] We can extrapolate backward, however, to get some sense of how the communities of Prouilhe, Madrid, and San Sisto may have been structured. Each monastery of nuns seems to have had a parallel community of friars whose superior confirmed the prioress elected by the nuns themselves. Dominic's solicitude for the nuns is reflected in words recorded in the chronicles of San Sisto: "My brothers, we really must build a monastery for the ladies, even if it means delaying building our own."[41] Within three years of Dominic's death, however, the question of care for the nuns became acute as the number of monasteries continued to

---

40. For a study of this rule, see Vicaire, *Saint Dominic and His Times*, appendix VIII, 428–35.

41. Barbara Beaumont, "The *Cura Monialium* Question," in *IDI* (International Dominican Information) 450 (March 2007): 64.

increase. A "Dominican family," however, existed from the beginning. There were lay brothers as well as priests. Laywomen and -men volunteers or associates, already at Prouilhe, helped to make the community's life possible. Today, the "family" comprises the friars, the nuns, active sisters, laity, and priestly fraternities.

When it seemed as if enough structure was in place, and Dominic and William would have been ready to go to preach to the pagans, Dominic's respect for the wishes of the pope and his concern for religious women had led him to attend to the needs of the Church. The pope, after all, had supported his dream and even expanded it. Who was he to say no? He could not help but recall the first foundation at Prouilhe and how supportive the women had been and continued to be to the preaching friars. If the Church needed him, Dominic would go, even though it meant the letting go, for now, of the cherished plan for his and William's becoming two friars preaching where the Word had not yet been heard.

THE CHAPTER OF 1221

Business in Rome completed, Dominic arrived back in Bologna at the end of May in time for the general chapter. The basic or fundamental constitutions had been established the previous year. But because the Order continued to grow, further organizational work was needed. A sense of provinces had already been in place as of 1220, but the understanding of what *province* meant continued to evolve. As of 1220 as well, Dominic was no longer "prior of the order" but Master of the Order. Abbot Matthew had come to the previous chapter as abbot, but as nomenclature continued to develop, left as prior of the province of France. The intermediate structures had become necessary due to the expansion of the preaching friars, and this expansion was a particular concern of the 1221 chapter.

The chapter of 1221 did not so much establish as acknowledge five provinces or regions: Spain, Provence, France, Lombardy, and the Roman province. Shortly thereafter, there would be Hungary, Teutonia, and England, to which regions this chapter sent brethren as well. Spain had the two houses of Segovia and Palencia in Castile and the monastery of nuns in Madrid. Provence by now had houses of brethren in Toulouse, Lyons, Montpellier, and the monastery of Prouilhe. In addition to the convent of St. Jacques in Paris, the province of France had convents in Rheims, Limoges, and Poitiers, such was the expansion of the Order in the short time of its existence. Lombardy boasted six houses, one of which was Bologna. The Roman province comprised Florence, Siena, and Santa Sabina as well as the monastery of San Sisto. Besides sending friars to Hungary, Scandinavia, Germany, and England, Brother Jacek (Hyacinth) was sent to Poland, where a house was established in Cracow. Given that the preaching in 1215 comprised a couple of brothers who had made profession to Dominic in Toulouse, the movement had grown beyond what Dominic could even have dreamed in 1217 when he dispersed the brothers. But in six years, the Order had spread throughout Europe, with about twenty houses of friars and three or four of nuns,[42] with the promise of even further expansion after the chapter of 1221. The basic structures of governance were now set in place and only needed further elaboration and clarification down the road.

---

42. The monasteries in whose founding Dominic was directly involved were those of Prouilhe, Madrid, and San Sisto in Rome. There was a previously existing monastery of nuns at San Esteban de Górmaz, between Osma and Caleruega, which nuns Dominic would have known and whom in 1218, while he was in Spain, may have made Dominican. This monastery itself moved to Caleruega in 1266. The monastery of St. Agnes in Bologna was only established after Dominic had died.

It is difficult to trace in detail and with precision the last couple of years of Dominic's life. It was increasingly centered in Bologna, where the chapters were held, and also involved business in Viterbo and Rome, as well as the continuing preaching, recruiting, establishment of new houses, and the tasks of governing. And Dominic's health was in decline. On several occasions, he had been seriously ill. Perhaps his own presentiments of declining health gave an urgency to the organizational challenge at hand that prompted his desire to step down. The chapter ended in early June 1221. Dominic continued the mission of evangelization from Bologna to Venice. He arrived back in Bologna from Venice by July 28, fatigued and ill, and he spent most of his time bedridden.

THE PASSING OF A SAINT

It is fitting that we pause before contemplating the death of this saint from Caleruega. Jordan of Saxony, who would succeed Dominic as the second Master of the Order of Preachers, wrote in his little book,

> Everybody was enfolded in the wide embrace of his charity, and since he loved everyone, everyone loved him. He made it his own business to rejoice with those who were rejoicing and to weep with those who wept. He was full of affection and gave himself utterly to caring for his neighbors and to showing sympathy for the unfortunate. (*Libellus*, no. 107)

Almost fifty years later, Etienne de Salagnac wrote, "Thus whoever passes a judgment free from envy will see that this saint was a canon by profession, a monk by the austerity of his life, an apostle by his preaching."[43] It is captivating to note how he was loved, how guided by the Spirit he allowed himself to be, how dependent on divine providence, how committed to the truth of the Catholic faith in his mission of evangelization, how deeply contemplative, humble, and committed to the poor and to voluntary poverty, with his gift for friendship, not self-promoting, always self-giving. Not yet fifty, the end was close at hand. His body was invaded with fever and dysentery, yet he continued fraternal conversations with young students in Bologna but, most of all, with his brother preachers and the novices at the convent of St. Nicholas.

By August, he was unable to stand. The brethren moved him from St. Nicholas, where the city's summer climate proved less than healthy for a sick man, to the Benedictine priory of Santa Maria in Monte to the south, where the air was fresher, but it was too late to reverse the course of events. On the morning of August 6, the feast of the Transfiguration, Dominic called for Brother Ventura, the prior,[44] who came with about twenty of the friars from St. Nicholas, with whom Dominic shared his last words. Jordan reports that Dominic confided in them, so symbolic of his humanness, what today we see as a touching moment, "I confess that I have not escaped from the imperfection of being more excited by the conversation of young women than by being talked at by old women" (*Libellus*, no. 92). Afterward, he worried that he had perhaps scandalized the novices. He then made his last confession. Ventura then confided to him that if he were to die there at Monte Mario, the monks there intended for the saint

---

43. Vicaire, *Saint Dominic and His Times*, 315.

44. Ventura of Verona had entered the Order in 1219 or 1220 and became prior in Bologna in 1221 toward the close of the chapter. He was later a witness in the canonization process.

to be buried there. Dominic exclaimed, "God forbid that I should be buried elsewhere than under the feet of my brethren. Carry me outside. Let me die on the roadside and then you will be able to bury me in your church."[45] And so the brethren carried him back to their convent of St. Nicholas.

To the end, Dominic thought of others, not of himself. In response to their tears, he consoled them, "Do not weep. I shall be of more use to you and bear more fruit for you after my death than I ever did in this life" (*Libellus*, no. 93). It was not false humility but a conviction about the intercessory power that resides with saints in heaven. It was now the time of waiting, something of an Advent before Dominic would be born again on the other shore. But on this side of that great divide, grief had set in. Dominic was ready. Toward evening, he gave his last instruction. "Begin," he said. The end was close at hand. Dominic knew. The community began. As they prayed, "Come to his aid, saints of God. Hasten, angels of the Lord. Receive his soul and offer it before the face of the Most High," Dominic breathed his last as paradise received his soul.

---

45. Vicaire, *Saint Dominic and His Times*, 373.

CHAPTER 5

AN AFTERWORD
The Preacher of Grace

Dominic's sanctity was undoubtedly recognized before he died. The monks at Maria in Monte could see it, as could his brother preachers, his wider family, and those whose lives were touched by his preaching. Yet it took time before his brethren took up the cause of his canonization. Twelve years passed. Brother Jordan of Saxony, whom Dominic had made a member of the Chapter of 1220 two months after his acceptance into the Order and who became provincial of Lombardy at the Chapter of 1221, succeeded Dominic as Master of the Order. In 1227, Cardinal Ugolino, who had provided Dominic with so much support and advice and would have been more than aware of Dominic's holiness, became Pope Gregory IX. He called to the attention of the friars what appeared to him as something of a neglect. Whether the thought of canonization came from some of the brethren or from the new pope, or was just in the air at the time, is difficult to determine.

Significant reconstruction of the church of St. Nicholas had left the tomb of Dominic outside and exposed to the elements. This made the brethren more aware of the need for a new tomb for their holy founder. What confronted the brethren in 1233, then, was the translation of St. Dominic to a new tomb, to take place at the time of the general chapter. Excitement, hope, and fear filled the air all at once. What would the opening of the tomb reveal? Signs of his sanctity? A foul odor? Grace or disgrace? The opening of the tomb, it was decided, would take place at night, between May 23 and 24. Undoubtedly with *angst* as well as deep prayer, the brethren were relieved when an incredible fragrance poured forth from the grave. They would have laughed and wept at the same time.[1] Praise God! This miracle of the overwhelming fragrance moved the story of Dominic from a translation of his bones to the canonization of a saint. One might say that God himself had opened the cause. The following year, after due process, Pope Gregory IX inserted St. Dominic into the calendar of saints and set August 5 as the date for his feast. Today, it is celebrated on August 8.

Dominic seems to have been competent, exemplary, and well liked. He embodied courage, compassion, and wisdom. People were drawn to him. This explains men's willingness to place their confidence in his preaching project, Diego's choice of him for the royal mission north, and the docile respect and affection shown him at the General Chapters. He was described as "always joyous and cheerful, except when moved to compassion at anyone's sorrows."[2] Jordan recalled, "By his cheerfulness he easily won the love of everybody. Without difficulty he found his way into people's hearts as soon as they saw him" (104). A Dominican friend of mine used the words *authentic, integrated,* and *joyful* to describe Dominic—a joyful friar, living what he

---

1. Vicaire, *Saint Dominic and His Times*, 384.
2. Sister Cecilia, quoted in *Lives of the Brethren of the Order of Preachers*, 89. Cecilia was a young nun of Santa Maria in Tempulo and among the first to move to the monastery at San Sisto. Later, she was one of the nuns sent to help establish the monastery in Bologna where she became prioress.

preached. It was no doubt painful for William of Montferrat to hear the word from Dominic concerning the pope's request about helping to establish a monastery at San Sisto. He knew Dominic only too well and knew what Dominic had to do, even at the cost to themselves. Discipleship and obedience took precedence over the friendship. No, discipleship was at the heart of their friendship, as friendship was, for Dominic, at the heart of his fraternal care. There are many stories of such magnanimous relationships within Dominican history. We need only to mention, already early on, the friendship of Jordan and Henry as well as that of Jordan and Diana.

Jordan of Saxony, who was elected to succeed Dominic upon Dominic's death, later wrote his little book, the *Libellus*, the story of the origins of the Order, while facts about it could still be recalled. In it, he relates the story of his own friendship with Henry, which they shared before they joined the Order as well as after. Jordan felt called to follow Dominic and persuaded Henry to come along with him. Here, too, there was the promise, the expectation, the hope, of their preaching together, not unlike the plan that Dominic and William had made. In Jordan's affectionate but humorous account of how he and Henry had been brought together into the Order, he said,

> While I [Jordan] was still speaking, we noticed another phrase [in the Book of Isaiah] a little further on in the text: "Let us stand together," and this seemed to be telling us never to desert each other, but to remain together in this special kind of companionship. (In connection with this text, he [Henry] wrote to me once from Cologne, when I was in Bologna, "What has happened now to 'Let us stand together?' You are in Bologna, and here am I in Cologne.") (nos. 70–71)

At the heart of spiritual friendship is Christian disciple-ship—the most precious thing that two friends can share. In telling the story in his "little book," Jordan expressed his love for Henry:

> But there is one thing I do know, and that is that there were only two people received to profession in the Order by him [Br. Reginald] in Paris, of whom I was the first, and the other was brother Henry, who was afterwards prior of Cologne, and who was, I think, my dearest friend in Christ. I loved him more than any-one else in the world. He really was a vessel of honor and grace. I do not remember ever seeing any more gracious creature in this life. (no. 66)

As time went on, Dominic's preaching became more like prayer. The active contemplative friar preached his prayer and prayed his preaching. But Dominic continued to preach—even up to the time of his death, which was a form of preaching as well, like the symbolic actions of Christ. Christ took children to himself, drove commercial business from the Temple, and washed the feet of his disciples. These prophetic symbolic acts pro-claimed God as much as anything Jesus ever said. The disciples would all have heard Jesus say in more than one way and on more than one occasion, "I have not come to be served but to serve" (Mark 10:45). What more likely stuck in their memories, how-ever, was his washing of their feet.

Still, there was no action on Jesus' part like his dying, giv-ing himself up to death on a cross, surrendering his life and will to his heavenly Father one last time. As both Thomas Aquinas[3]

---

3. Thomas Aquinas, *Summa Theologiae*, III, q. 46, a. 4, quoting Augustine: "The tree upon which were fixed the members of Him dying was even the chair of the Master teaching."

and Catherine of Siena[4] beautifully put it, the cross was Jesus' pulpit, his professor's podium. From it he preached and the action reverberated around the world. Likewise for Dominic's dying. If what his mother heard while he was still in the womb, that his voice would be heard around the world, so his dying was a preaching that was heard and his parting words made sense to everyone, namely, that he would be of more use to them after he died than he had been while living among them. While it would be hard to let him go, they knew that the words reflected his deep faith, the foundation for his life of preaching.

ST. DOMINIC OF CALERUEGA, CONTEMPLATIVE PREACHER

Sometimes a person is only known in hindsight. Was he a saint, a holy man, or just ordinary? What portrait of this preaching friar might we now sketch? It would be difficult to say whether Dominic's contemplative nature or his gift for preaching was the more characteristic feature. In him, they were inseparable. To be a preacher was to be a contemplative, and to be truly contemplative was to allow that which boils inside to boil over.[5] There could be no authentic contemplation without the handing on of it to others and vice versa. How did the gift of contemplation manifest itself through him?

---

4. Catherine of Siena, *The Letters of Catherine of Siena*, trans. Suzanne Noffke, OP (Tempe, AZ: Arizona Center for Medieval and Renaissance Studies, 2007), vol. III, letters T216, p. 50, and T316, p. 330.

5. "Boiling" and "boiling over," (*bullitio* and *ebullitio*) are an image that Meister Eckhart uses to talk about the dynamic life of the Trinity and its flowing over into the act of creation, which is an image that can also portray contemplation bearing fruit in action or preaching. See Richard Woods, OP, *Eckhart's Way* (Wilmington, DE: Michael Glazier, 1986), 89–91. Also see Bernard McGinn, *The Mystical Thought of Meister Eckhart, The Man From Whom God Hid Nothing* (New York: Crossword Publishing, 2001).

Caleruega itself would have been a natural habitat for fostering a contemplative life. Growing up in the country, a rural village, invites it. His choice of the life of a canon in Osma demonstrated it. It was already there. His love of the Scriptures, those prized works of St. Matthew and St. Paul that he always carried with him, nourished it. Why choose the conferences of John Cassian, that monk who, along with his friend Germanus, brought the wisdom of the desert fathers to the West? Can one truly understand Dominic apart from those conferences that he kept by his bedside in Osma? The Gospel according to Mark, like those of Matthew and Luke, pictures Jesus getting up early in the morning to go off to a lonely place to pray (Mark 1:35–39). Dominic also found times for solitary prayer and for the celebration of the Divine Office and Eucharist. The disciples then came to Jesus to say, "Everyone is searching for you." I would have asked them to wait a minute; these precious moments of solitude are not easily gained. But no, Jesus responds immediately: "Let us go on to the next towns, that I may preach there also; for that is what I came out to do." I wonder what went through Dominic's heart and mind as he heard and meditated on those words from Scripture. They have made me think what a wonderful Dominican Jesus would have made! But would Dominic not more likely have thought, How might I be more like Christ? If only I could follow more faithfully in his footsteps.

Still, there is more. What were those nine ways of praying that a later disciple felt the desire to transcribe and draw?[6] These were Dominic the wholehearted contemplative and wholehearted preacher, not half contemplative and half preacher. The

---

6. Of unknown authorship, written down somewhere between 1260–88, considered to manifest the actual practice of St. Dominic. See Simon Tugwell, OP, *The Nine Ways of Prayer of Saint Dominic* (Dublin: Dominican Publications, 1978); also see *Early Dominicans* (New York: Paulist Press, 1982), 94–103. Also see Leonard Boyle, OP, "The Ways of Prayer of St. Dominic," *AFP* 64 (1994): 5–17.

Shema of his people must have rung deeply in Jesus' heart and shaped his life of union with his heavenly Father. The Jewish people were admonished not to let those words ("Hear, O Israel: The LORD is our God, the LORD alone. You shall love the LORD your God with all your heart, and with all your soul, and with all your might.") diminish in their awareness and thus were instructed to "recite them to your children and talk about them when you are at home and when you are away, when you lie down and when you rise" (Deut 6:4–9). Dominic made incarnate this injunction in his nine ways of prayer.

Dominic is depicted in them as praying, whether bowing humbly, or lying prostrate, or using the discipline, sometimes gazing at the crucifix while kneeling, or standing reverently upright, at times with arms outstretched, or with arms lifted up high toward heaven, at times sitting, or when walking on a journey. When walking, he saw God in nature. When he was reading, the Word of God came through the Scriptures. In front of the crucifix or the Blessed Sacrament, he saw God, he loved God, and he spoke to God. In his preaching, he spoke about the God he loved and the God who loves. His preaching ought to have been listed as his tenth way of praying, for at times it was difficult to tell where one left off and the other began.

It was reported that in his prayer, Dominic sometimes moved directly from reading (*lectio*) to contemplation (*contemplatio*). The tradition of the time emphasized four movements in the symphony of prayer. Beginning with the prayerful *reading* of a text (*lectio*), especially but not necessarily a biblical text, the symphony moved to a *pondering* of the text (*meditatio*), a bringing it from the mind into the heart in the tradition of the desert fathers. From there it moved to *oratio*—*prayer* proper, speaking to God, engaging God more directly, no longer thinking about God but talking to God and letting God speak—and finally to contemplation (*contemplatio*), where we not only let God speak but let God be God in us; this could also be called a grace-filled receptivity to a mindful wordless interior stillness in which we get ourselves out of the way so that God might rush in. We might say that if the prayer began "from below," it ended coming "from above." Metaphors for God often depict God as either "Above" or "Within," yet it has also been stated that for St. Augustine "'Within' *is* 'above.'"[7] The "Above" is "Within" and the "Within" is "Above." So it was for Dominic's nine or ten or dozen ways of praying. He certainly would have taken to heart St. Paul's instruction to the Thessalonians: "Pray without ceasing" (1 Thess 5:17). Paul was obviously a model for Dominic's own contemplative heart.

For us today, however, the word *contemplative* can be misunderstood. We are inclined to separate people into the contemplatives and the actives, or the mystics and the prophets, or the be-ers and the doers, rather than realize that contemplation and action, prayer and ministry, are more akin to inhaling and exhaling, two things that cannot be separated, although even that image is not Dominican enough. This is why Meister Eckhart and Catherine of Siena see it more like "becoming pregnant" and "giving birth."[8] You don't get one without the other. The goal of becoming pregnant is to give birth, and one can't give birth without becoming pregnant. To attempt the handing on or sharing (*tradere*) while neglecting contemplation (*contemplari*) is like assuming that one can give birth without becoming pregnant.

---

7. Denys Turner, *The Darkness of God, Negativity in Christian Mysticism* (Cambridge, UK: University Press, 1995), 100.

8. In his German sermons, Meister Eckhart placed great emphasis on the theme of the birth of the Word in the ground of the soul. Catherine of Siena wrote, "If a woman has conceived a child but never brings it to birth for people to see, her husband will consider himself childless." (*The Dialogue*, trans. Suzanne Noffke [New York: Paulist Press, 1980], chap. 11, p. 45)

Both Catherine and Eckhart were Dominican mystics of the four-teenth century, but it is no wonder that such images came to their minds, having grown up in Dominican soil. Thus, it is no wonder that Eckhart, in contrast to centuries of spiritual biblical inter-pretation before him, saw Martha as the more spiritually mature of the two in the account of Mary and Martha in chapter 10 of the Gospel of Luke.[9] To be contemplative does not necessarily mean to withdraw from the world, as beautiful an approach to living a contemplative life that may be, but it was not what prov-idence had in store for Dominic, whose contemplation would be more itinerant. To be contemplative means to "live in the tem-ple" (Latin *con* or *cum* + *templum*), or again, if we were to borrow from Dominic's son Eckhart, to live in the ground of one's soul, to be grounded, to be centered, or perhaps to stay with St. Paul, whom Dominic so loved, to live in the temple but realize that "you are God's temple…and God's temple is holy, and you are that temple" (1 Cor 3:16–17). In other words, being contempla-tive does not necessarily mean withdrawal from the world, a life devoid of pastoral concerns, or a less apostolic life. Dominic was an itinerant contemplative.

A second major misconception that we moderns have about living contemplatively is that it is akin to a life of leisure. I myself once had a notion along that line, until a Dominican brother of mine and I founded a Dominican "ashram" or contemplative Dominican house. I thought that my life would then be given what it deserved: love, joy, peace, patience, kindness, goodness, faithfulness, gentleness, and self-control (Gal 5:22). I was sur-prised by sadness. What did I expect? Thomas Keating used the image of bringing fresh spring water into a garbage can. What

---

9. See Meister Eckhart, *Sermons and Treatises*, trans. M. O'C. Walshe, vol. 1 (London: Watkins Pub., 1979), sermon 9, pp. 79–90. Also see *Meister Eckhart, Teacher and Preacher*, ed. Bernard McGinn (New York: Paulist Press, 1986), sermon 86, 338–45.

happens? What rises to the surface? The garbage. So the beginning of a meditative life allows an inner quiet to release what otherwise we ignore or run from in the midst of busying ourselves about many things. What we then see inside ourselves: pride, covetousness, lust, gluttony, anger, envy, and sloth. Dominic read and knew his Paul. He would have understood why words like aridity, darkness, desolation, emptiness, nights of the soul, and unknowing would be associated with the contemplative or mystical life. After all, upon what was he meditating while standing before the crucifix? What was the soul he poured out during his well-known all-night vigils?

St. Dominic was not only a contemplative, however; he was a contemplative preacher. What was it about preaching that gave him this identity? Preaching carries with it other words, like *gospel, truth, the Word,* and *Jesus Christ, crucified and raised from the dead.* Preaching is never a solitary act. It respects a "hearer." It recognizes that the hearer has a context from which he or she comes. One wants to reach that hearer with something vitally important to the preacher, something heartfelt, something deeply believed with "all one's mind, all one's heart, all one's soul." Preaching has to do with proclamation. It is not a one-way street; the proclaimer has to sense the vibrations in the heart of the hearers in order to know whether he is genuinely communicating. As St. Augustine wrote, "There are two things which all treatment of the scriptures is aiming at: a way to discover what needs to be understood, and a way to put across to others what has been understood."[10]

That which is proclaimed is the *gospel.* When we hear the word, many think of the four Gospels, and they are our source for

---

10. Saint Augustine, *Teaching Christianity* (*De Doctrina Christiana*), trans. Edmund Hill, OP (Hyde Park, NY: New City Press, 1996), Bk. 1, chap. 1, p. 106.

sure. But they are not the gospel itself. They are the gospel as written, and written according to Matthew, according to Mark, and so on. But those Gospels, the basis for the proclamation, are called Gospels because they contain the gospel, that is, the story of another preacher, teacher, and healer: the story of our Lord Jesus Christ. And who would this Jesus have been for Dominic, to whom he had turned over his life, way back before he knew it, at his baptism? It was this Jesus and this Jesus' gospel that Dominic preached. Yes, it was the story of the life, death, and resurrection of Jesus Christ, but it was also what Jesus himself preached, what Mark and Paul both refer to as the "gospel of God" (Mark 1:14; Rom 1:1). In other words, the gospel is God's story, too: who God was, who God is, who God will be; that God of love and mercy and infinite compassion. What will become of sinners? Dominic had asked in his prayer. For Dominic, preaching was linked with salvation: it had to be salvific. The Constitutions of the Order would later say that the Order was established for the sake of preaching *and* the salvation of souls.[11] The one could not be separated out from the other. Preaching had to do with the life of the soul. One had to proclaim a word that would rescue that soul from isolation, from loneliness, from embitterment, from self-destruction.

Thus the gospel, at its core, tells us of a God who loves, who saves, who cares. This was the God that Dominic had met in his own prayer, and among the poor, and when hearing the confessions of sinners. It is God's story, God's gospel, the gospel that Jesus preached, the gospel that became so embodied or incarnate in Jesus of Nazareth that it is the gospel of Jesus Christ, the gospel about Jesus, the gospel for whom Jesus gave his life. Preaching is

---

11. "The Fundamental Constitution," chap. 2 in *The Book of Constitutions and Ordinations of the Brothers of the Order of Preachers* (Dublin: Dominican Publications, 2012).

good news, an *evangelium*, even when it tells the truth about sin, and righteousness and judgment, as the Gospel of John portrays the post-Resurrection work of the Holy Spirit (John 16:8).

That brings us to Truth. I'm not sure whether today I would choose that word, although it is one of the three primary mottos of the Order of Preachers. Truth can have many connotations. There are those who think they have the truth, all the truth, and nothing but the truth. There are those who hit people over the head with truth. There are those who absolutely know the truth. So I'm never sure from where one comes when they hold up the banner of truth. Yet there are the seekers, those whose journey in life seems to be to pursue the truth. Gandhi himself titled his autobiography *The Story of my Experiments with Truth*. South Africa, in recent times, had to come through Truth and Reconciliation. Certainly truth is something we all value. Yet the flavor may be better carried with the word *wisdom*—*sapientia* in Latin, *sophia* in Greek, and *hokmah* in Hebrew. One who loves wisdom is a philosopher. Truth carries with it a certain amount of baggage, yet can emerge with its head held high. The Holy Spirit is the Spirit of Truth in the Gospel of John (John 14:17;15:26; 16:13), and in his last discourse, Jesus prays to his heavenly Father for his friends, his disciples: "Sanctify them in the truth; your word is truth" (John 17:17). One can speak of the power of truth in contrast to manipulative or exploitative forms of power. So let's savor truth—the kind of truth that we find in the gospel—the kind of truth that so energized Dominic that he gave himself wholeheartedly to proclaiming it—the kind of truth that he saw in the Catholic faith.

Truth can never be identified with one avenue alone. "In my Father's house there are many dwelling places" (John 14:2). This is not to say that truth is relative. No, there *is* truth. God *is*

Truth. But, as St. Thomas says, there is Truth but also many truths.[12] In the search for Truth, it is God whom we seek, and whom we come to understand as being incomprehensible even if intelligible. Truth eludes us at the same time it captures us. While it is Truth that binds us together within the Order, it is also Truth that diversifies or even divides us. We can be passionate about what really is real, what really is right, what really matters, but our insights, our perspectives, our angles vary. Each one's passion for truth can put him or her at odds with someone else whose desire is just as sincere. Father Ralph Powell, a wise Dominican, once said, "It's hard to see the whole picture if you're inside the frame." None of us has the whole picture. For Dominic, and for a Preacher, the search for truth brings us to the Word—the eternal Word incarnate in Jesus Christ, the Word enfleshed in Holy Scripture, the Word embedded in the community of the faithful, the Word proclaimed in preaching.

Dominic's ministry, and that of his future family of preachers, was and is a ministry of the Word. The Word was at the center of Dominic's life. This is Jesus Christ. This is the sacred text. This is the ecclesial community in which one finds the Word proclaimed and celebrated in the Eucharist. This is why we find one of the ways of prayer of St. Dominic as that of praying explicitly with the Word. This is why he always made the effort to be sure that his preaching movement would remain in the midst of the Church, which is where it had begun, with the visit of Dominic and Bishop Fulk to Innocent III, even if the Order also pulled the

---

12. Thomas Aquinas, *Summa Theologiae*, I, q. 6, a. 4: "Everything therefore is called good from the divine goodness, as from the first exemplary, effective and final principle of all goodness. Nevertheless, everything is called good by reason of the similitude of the divine goodness belonging to it, which is formally its own goodness, whereby it is denominated good. And so of all things there is one goodness, and yet many goodnesses." In an analogous fashion, q. 16, a. 6, quoting a gloss: "As from one man's face many likenesses are reflected in a mirror, so many truths are reflected from the one divine truth."

Church in new directions, just as Dominic did. Dominic made his home in the Word. He was at home with the Word. I have sometimes said that a Dominican is most himself or herself, most who we are, when we preach. We can let the truth about ourselves be revealed in ways that otherwise we may guard. That's who I am. That's who he was—a preaching friar.

I cannot verify every detail of this story since some of it I received by word of mouth. Father Samuel Mazzuchelli was a loyal son of St. Dominic. He was an Italian missionary, one of the first Dominicans to come to that world that had been so new to Old Europe. Father Edward Fenwick and confreres from England had established the Order in the eastern United States in 1805. Mazzuchelli arrived in 1828 and was commissioned to do missionary work in the region of Michigan, Wisconsin, and the Mississippi Valley. In 1847, he established a community of Dominican sisters in Sinsinawa, Wisconsin, his own Prouilhe. He had also attempted to establish a province of friars for the Midwest, which was absorbed into the eastern province of St. Joseph in 1849. Samuel was filled with a missionary spirit and at home with the Word. He died in 1864.[13]

Father Timothy Sparks, OP (d. 2001), an incredibly charitable friar and member of the central province of St. Albert the Great, was very dedicated to the Sinsinawa Dominican sisters, and thus as well to Father Samuel Mazzuchelli, whose cause for canonization was something he promoted. Father Sparks was also an internationally known Josephologist who had published many articles on St. Joseph. Nothing would have made him happier than having St. Joseph's name included in the canon of the Mass, as it now is, except perhaps the canonization of Father Samuel.

---

13. Mary Nona McGreal, OP, *Samuel Mazzuchelli: American Dominican* (Notre Dame, IN: Ave Maria Press, 2005).

Thus it came as good news, according to the account I had heard, that a possible miracle had been obtained through the intercession of Father Samuel. Two such miracles were needed for progress toward canonization. Thus it was with some consternation, at least to Father Sparks, that the person had *also* prayed to St. Joseph! To whom then could credit for the miracle go? Thus Father Sparks wrote a learned article titled "Saint Joseph, an Unobstructed Cause of Grace"—an instrumental cause to be sure but nevertheless a channel of grace. Therefore, Father Samuel could be credited with the miracle. St. Joseph would want it that way.

I never read the article, nor am I sure that the details of the story are not apocryphal, but the title of the so-called article fascinated me. What greater compliment could be given one than to see that person as an unobstructed source of grace, a channel of the Holy Spirit, channeling the Spirit without placing any obstacle in the Spirit's path? Of course, the Spirit can do powerful things even with obstructed channels, but to be without obstruction! For virtue to have so won out over everyday vice! This would be the miracle of grace indeed, and it is that miracle that St. Dominic was. This unobstructed channel of grace simply saw himself as a servant of the preaching, and it was the preaching that was important, not the preacher, not himself. He was a contemplative preacher, a preaching friar, a preacher of grace.

PATHS TO HOLINESS

Obedience is the only vow that Dominicans profess. On the other hand, since he was a mendicant, voluntary poverty was close to Dominic's heart. If we think of chastity as the capacity for relationships, Dominic was well schooled in the art of friendship. Too often we tend to define or understand religious life in contrast to marriage. But this does a disservice to both. Christian sacramental marriage is an incredible way of giving oneself to another and to Christ. It is a sacrament, but we don't contrast it with the sacrament of Orders. Indeed, it is possible for someone to be both married and a priest. Marriage has to be understood in and of itself. Likewise religious life is a distinct Christian call. It is not intrinsically related to priesthood, although some orders of men are clerical, such as the Dominican. In Dominic's time, the call to preach required priesthood, although much lay preaching also took place. Men and women in religious life are called to a special way of loving, of giving themselves to others, a distinct way of turning one's life over to God. The vows are not seen as restrictive but as paths to holiness and, for Dominic, central to the Holy Preaching. Let us consider obedience first, since it is the hinge for all the vows that Preachers make.[14]

OBEDIENCE: For a friar, the formula for solemn profession is:

> I, Brother ____, make profession and promise obedience to God, to blessed Mary, and to blessed Dominic, and to you brother ____, Master of the Order of Friars Preachers and to your successors, according to the rule of blessed Augustine and the institutions of the Friars Preachers, that I will be obedient to you and your successors until death.[15]

There is no need to make explicit the commitments to voluntary evangelical poverty and celibate chastity. Dominican obedience, like the other vows, has a particular stamp of its own. It

---

14. I have written on aspects of the vows elsewhere. See *Letters to My Brothers and Sisters* (Dublin: Dominican Publications, 1996), 34–41, 65–69, 122–26, 137–42.

15. *The Book of Constitutions and Ordinations of the Brothers of the Order of Preachers*, nos. 199, 211.

is not an abandonment of the use of one's intelligence. Accommodations are made through the structure of dispensations, an innovation among rules for religious life.

From a spiritual point of view, which is always the starting point for any of the vows, it is a question of conforming one's life to Christ—again, something laid out by St. Paul in his letters: it involves the asceticism of blending one's will with that of Christ, so that the two shall be one. As Jesus himself modeled in his petition to his heavenly Father, "Not what I want, but what you want" (Mark 14:36). At the heart of the vow is the brother's desire to conform his will to that of Christ's through the power of the Holy Spirit who has been given us. It is a question of becoming an unobstructed channel of the Spirit—just as Dominic himself became as the twists and turns of his life unfolded. What he became and was called to do was not what he would have expected when he left Caleruega to study in Palencia, nor when he joined the cathedral chapter in Osma, nor when he even first began to preach with Diego. Providence has ways of its own.

Obedience is not simply a gracious attentiveness to the role of a superior, although that is certainly involved, but rather hearing the will of the brothers to whom we are vowed in our common life and of the chapter as the basic structure of governance. There are plenty of opportunities to choose between willfulness and detachment as one grows in the conformity of one's life with that of Christ. Obedience is not so far removed from the moral virtue of prudence or the Spirit's gift of wisdom. Everything is geared toward a life of charity. Prior to Dominic, the monastic tradition had spoken already of religious life as a school for learning charity. Indeed, it is true. The process of conforming our wills, letting go of attachments and ego, is a lifelong journey that the vows are intended to support. When a friar makes profession, the one who receives the vow asks, "What do you seek?" The response is "God's mercy and yours." We physically place our hands in the hands of our brother-superiors. This is a sign that we place ourselves in the hands of our brothers. The root Latin words for obedience tell us that obedience is learning the art of listening, something that we must be able to do before we can hear God's voice, or our neighbor's voice, or the cry of the poor. This is deeply connected to living contemplatively.

Some say that Dominic was given the gift of governance, but was it not that destiny placed certain things in his hands? Diego asked him to accompany him on a journey. He did not know where it would lead. It was not the Nordic countries to which he was being invited by the Lord. Diego died. Bishop Fulk invited and encouraged him to establish the Holy Preaching in his diocese. Dominic responded. Pope Innocent challenged him to think big, bigger than he had ever thought, to have a vision beyond Toulouse. Dominic thought of Peter and of Paul and dispersed his preaching friars. It was about the mission. It was about the preaching. What began in Osma came to fulfillment in Rome. His desire was to preach, to evangelize the unevangelized, with a friar-friend, but San Sisto got in the way. The Order came first, before his own will, before friendship for which he had such a gift. Destiny? Providence? The gift of governance? Yes, but it was called forth from within him. It was not a gift he sought or knew he had. It was his charitable nature that made him succeed as a leader. He allowed himself to be an unobstructed channel of grace. Thus, the gift of governance was his. He tried to step down, to hand it on, but his was a life of service. His vocation was that of a preacher, a preaching friar, his desire to go and preach in the company of a friend. But it was a larger task to which God had called him. His call was not to be a bishop, nor a monk, but the "humble servant of preaching" (*praedicationis humilis minister*). He was a contemplative at heart, and a missionary too, and he has taught us what it means to be contemplative missionaries, to contemplate and to hand on the fruits of one's contemplation.

A friar friend of mine highlighted this responsiveness and receptivity of Dominic to what was asked of him. As he put it, "What is often taken as Dominic's creativity is his mode of responding when given a task to do." He willingly accompanied his bishop on the journeys north. The community at Prouihle was established in response to a need to care for women converts. At the request of Bishop Fulk, he centered his preaching in Toulouse. He consulted his brethren in adopting the Rule of St. Augustine. He was attuned to the signs of the times. The dispersal of his brethren was in response to the awareness that the future of Toulouse hung in a balance. What would become of the preaching if they had remained there? What was most visionary about Dominic was perhaps his choosing to send his brothers to the intellectual centers of Europe. Even here he was responding to a need. In all that he did, Dominic was an obedient son of the Church. Dominic's obedience consisted in such actions or responses as these. Even when he had chosen at their first general chapter to resign, he acquiesced to the wish of his brothers. Dominic was an obedient man. Perhaps his greatest personal desire was to be a missionary, but his brothers and the request of Pope Honorius to establish a convent at San Sisto came first. He never did get to visit far foreign lands.

Did Dominic ever get angry? Was he ever disappointed? What did he feel when John of Navarre refused to go to Paris without any money in his pocket? Was he ever annoyed with the behavior of his brothers? Certainly he loved them and prayed for them, but that does not mean he himself did not require the school of charity in order to advance in wisdom, age, and grace. Dominic was known for his charity, which was certainly grace at work in his life, but not one so given to him that it did not require stretching on his part. He knew what obedience meant when he put the Order in *their* hands. Yet he was able to remain the gentle Master and they all loved him in return. But learning to love does not come cheap, and one never knows the suffering in someone else's heart. Dominic was a lover, but one along the lines that his St. Paul had outlined for him in Paul's First Letter to the Corinthians, chapter 13.

Certainly Dominic experienced many disappointments but remained trusting in God. One can also speak in general and of religious life in particular as a school of disappointments. It is not so much whether there will be disappointments in life, but what we do with them. They can make us cynics, or they can help us to become contemplatives. Whether country, or Church, or community, or spouse, life will offer us disappointments enough. So it was with Dominic, the disappointment he must have experienced as he heard the final word about the marriage that he and Diego were supposed to arrange, the disappointment at discovering the depth and extent of the heresy in southern France, the sad news of Diego's death, disappointments in the preaching, Pope Innocent's call for a crusade, the laborious years of waiting for the war to come to an end, the death of parents however he may have heard, and the death of Simon de Montfort and what it might portend, the challenges in founding an order, the desire to preach with William delayed and delayed, the awareness that not all the brothers valued or saw poverty as he did. But cynicism seems never to have touched his soul, but rather only the joy that is an effect of a contemplative life. Aquinas would teach that joy is an effect of the virtue of charity.[16] In the face of what life puts in our paths, eventually we all have to decide which road to take—that toward a more contemplative living, or that of a more cynical life.

Obedience, in the end, is a commitment to a way of life, in this case, the way of a Preacher. What is required of the friar and a community so that the preaching might flourish? Dominic must have pondered this question as the brothers gathered to put together their constitutions for the first time. What will make community work? What must its foundation be? I suspect that Christ Jesus is the answer to which Dominic kept coming back— the following after Jesus (*sequela Jesu*). To be a Preacher is to be like Christ. Thus, we must more and more conform ourselves to Christ. Again, St. Paul tells us, "Let the same mind be in you that was in Christ Jesus" (Phil 2:5). To desire to put one's life at the service of Christ, however, means to learn the prayer, "Not my will." This doesn't mean we don't have free will or that having desires is wrong, but the ultimate desire of our heart is to love Christ Jesus—and to love him crucified. As in Paul's great hymn in his Letter to the Philippians (2:6–11), there is a certain self-emptying at the heart of the gospel and at the heart of the spiritual life. Obedience is self-emptying applied to our wills. Chastity is self-emptying with respect to the tendency toward possessiveness in relationships. Poverty is self-emptying with respect to the "things" of this world. To be emptied of self so as to be filled with Christ. To draw on an insight from Erich Fromm, is my life more focused on "having" or "being"?[17] We all want to have our way, we want our friend to be "ours," and there are those things that are so much with us that they shape our identities, some of these being our theologies and opinions. There is nothing wrong with

16. Thomas Aquinas, *Summa Theologiae*, II–II, q. 28, a. 1, 4.
17. Erich Fromm, *To Have or To Be?* (New York: Continuum International, 2004).

having, but the Preacher's focus needs to be on being. It is who we *are* and who Dominic *was* that preaches. Dominican obedience is at heart a desire for holiness.

POVERTY: Voluntary poverty is distinct from involuntary poverty, that is, socioeconomic poverty. It is also distinct from poverty of spirit to which all Christians are called. At the heart of voluntary poverty is the common life. For Dominic, it was all about the preaching. Common life had been lived before, in the monasteries, but some of them had also become wealthy. Dominican poverty would mean a shared life, a simple life, a mendicant life, an evangelical life. It would be, above all, a Preacher's life.

A *shared life*: Everything would be held in common. There would be no private ownership of goods. The biblical model would be, "Now the whole group of those who believed were of one heart and soul, and no one claimed private ownership of any possessions, but everything they owned was held in common" (Acts 4:32). It was already a reality prescribed in the Rule of St. Augustine. It meant dependence on the community and interdependence within the community. It was what later (in the nineteenth century) would be seen as a utopian ideal lived among the brethren: from each according to his ability, to each according to his needs. For Dominic, it was not a utopian vision at all but a way of life, the way of the Preacher.

A *simple life*: Everything could be held in common and yet a monastery might be rich. Thus, the goal of evangelical poverty was also to live only with what one needs, without needs being defined by the world outside or, in our times, by a consumer society whose marketing is based on the creation of needs. Rather, the needs would be defined by the preaching in light of the practice of mendicancy. The life was to give witness to the gospel. As we have seen, Dominic placed a high priority on the practice of poverty, even though its practice continued to evolve from what Dominic himself originally envisioned. This poverty was voluntary but essential, to be embraced by all who were called to share in the preaching life. Catherine of Siena saw voluntary poverty as a path to holiness: "Voluntary poverty where the world is concerned enriches our soul and frees it from servitude; it makes us kind and mild; it takes away our empty faith and trust in transitory things and gives us living faith and true hope."[18]

A *mendicant life*: Everything was held in common, but from where did it all come? The early friars were beggars. In the beginning, Dominic preferred that they beg for only enough to get through a day; with time, they were able to beg in order to have a storehouse for the days ahead. Dominic, always willing to be consultative among the brothers, clearly preferred a life of almost absolute poverty. It would be a frugal life.[19] Begging reminds one not only of one's dependency on the others, but upon God. The Order most thrives when the life of poverty is genuinely lived. When the common life and that of voluntary poverty declined, so did the Order. For Dominic and Diego, poverty and the preaching went together. One without the other would cripple whichever leg on which one was left to stand. Dominic preferred not only itinerant poverty but also conventual poverty, but in true obedience, he left his wishes in the hands of his brethren. But poverty was part of the way of the

---

18. Letter T67, to the convent of Passignano of Valle Ombrosa, *The Letters of Catherine of Siena*, vol. 3, pp. 3–4.

19. Vladimir Koudelka, on Dominic, writes, "That meant travelling on foot instead of riding on horseback. Dominic himself was an indefatigable walker...a calculation of the distances he covered after the foundation of the order gives us an average of forty to fifty kilometers a day [about twenty-five to thirty miles]....But the most troublesome aspect of this way of life was spending the night in hospices for poor pilgrims, teeming with fleas, lice, and bugs, to such an extent that the friars were often unable to sleep a wink" (p. 36).

Preacher from the beginning. One could hardly find anything more at the core of the Holy Preaching.

An evangelical life: The apostolic life (*vita apostolica*) was the life lived by the apostles, which was not only a life of preaching and itineracy but the common life as that had come to be understood in earlier centuries.[20] But it was also the way of Jesus, who had nowhere to lay his head and who had to pray for daily bread. Religious life—indeed, any life—truly thrives when it places its trust in God. Poverty was about a spirituality of trust. "Blessed are those who...." Just as the beatitudes have inspired humanity through the ages, so Dominic would have found them in his cherished Gospel of St. Matthew. He had given away his parchments in Palencia so even his Gospel was no longer "his." Evangelical poverty is also Christian poverty and merges in connection to the involuntarily poor. "I was hungry..." (Matt 25:31–46). Poverty never became so divisive that there was a division in the Order. The unity of the Order is one of three things in particular that the friars value because they connect us so with Dominic himself. The other two are the religious habit and the evolutionary character of our Constitutions. The habit of the friar connects him with Dominic, and the evolutionary character of the constitutions has allowed him to adjust to the signs of the times throughout the ages.

CHASTITY: In our times, chastity may seem out of sync with the contemporary world. In the Middle Ages, it was common for a member of a family to be "offered" to the Church, the tradition of oblates. So whether Dominic thought much about the implications of a celibate life we may not know. What we do know is that he valued it. It was not so much taking something

---

20. Marie-Dominique Chenu, OP, "Monks, Canons, and Laymen in Search of the Apostolic Life," in *Nature, Man, and Society in the Twelfth Century* (Chicago: The University of Chicago Press, 1968), 202–38.

as part of a package but being attentive to how the package is wrapped. Although there were witnesses to his chaste life at the time of his canonization, one interesting story lingers that indicates both Dominic's commitment to the life of chastity and also his awareness of the sacrifice it entails. As I wrote earlier, he is reported to have said in his last confession, "I confess that I have not escaped from the imperfection of being more excited by the conversation of young women than by being talked at by old women." The story lingers because Dominic's humanity breaks through—just as it does in the story of his relationships in general, with the brethren, with the nuns, with Diana d'Andalò, with William of Montferrat, with Bishops Diego and Fulk. Dominic had a capacity for relationship, which is at the heart of a chaste life.

Chastity is not so much about our sexuality as it is about being human with others. It teaches us what relationships are all about. Ann Willets, a Dominican sister from Sinsinawa, Wisconsin, likes to say in her preaching, "It is not that we are human beings striving to be holy, but that we are holy people learning to be human." Humanness is what it's all about. As Thomas Aquinas taught us, and as Aristotle did before him, we can sin against humanness by excess and by defect. We can be careless about our sexuality, our relationships, our friendships, or we can be overly protective so as not to commit a sin of the flesh. This is what led Gerald Vann, a great English Dominican and spiritual writer, to say in his introduction to the letters of Jordan to Diana,

> Just as foolish direction can ruin a young man's health, both physically and psychologically, in the sacred name of asceticism or religious fervor; just as a false theory of obedience can give him a wholly wrong outlook on

life by training him to identify the ideal with the unnatural; just as he may have his youthful gaiety extinguished in him for the sake of a stuffy decorum, or his individuality quenched by the imposition of a common pattern, a sort of pseudo-personality; so too his emotional nature, his heart, may be wholly repressed and smothered, the lid firmly screwed down, while all his energies are directed to the avoidance of wrongdoing, so that he ends in a sort of irreproachable vacuum. (Sometimes this last is justified on the grounds of playing for safety: but safety for what?... Our Lord did not say 'I am come that ye may have safety, and have it more abundantly'. Some of us would indeed give anything to feel safe, about our life in this world as in the next, but we cannot have it both ways: safety or life, we must choose.)[21]

Chastity, like all the vows, is a question of balance, of living a balanced, integrated life. It tells us that persons are important and we are called on to respect their dignity—whether this be in community, in ministry or in friendships. The "other" is important. So celibate chastity is not a cerebral, nonaffective way of living, but rather a contemplative approach to all of life. Dominic seems to have been that kind of man, one in whose presence one felt blessed. This describes another Dominican, now deceased, Sister Marygrace Peters of the Houston Dominican sisters. To be in her presence was a blessed thing. All Dominicans can tell the stories of our friendships. Although there are times of loneliness, we are not prone to it. The life is too rich. There's the preaching, the family, the friends, and our Lord. In the fourteenth century, there was

---

21. Gerald Vann, OP, "Introduction," in *To Heaven with Diana*, 40.

the later movement, known as the Friends of God, that surrounded another preaching friar, Meister Eckhart. God was Dominic's friend. As Bede Jarrett, another eminent English Dominican, wrote in his own life of Dominic, commenting on the death of Dominic: "He was a friend to them all, but you feel as you read that *his* friend was God."[22] So were his brothers, and his sisters, and William, and on and on. Chastity enables one to live a full life. As in any way of life, one does not focus on what one does not have but on what one receives, and it is the hundredfold promised by Jesus.

There is much about Dominic's personal life that we do not know. Not so much that he was a private person, for he was a very public man, but that he never sought to be the center of attention. As an old song goes, "Love is something if you give it away, you've got to give it away," and so it was with Dominic. His life was his to be given away and chastity provided him the arena within which to do it. In our day and age, one has to learn chastity, grow into it, for it is not a cultural value reinforced by social norms. If anything, perhaps the opposite is true. But for Dominic, it was who he was, and it was about love. All true love is chaste love, whether conjugal or celibate. One's sexuality is put at the service of the gospel, like the rest of one's life. To quote St. Paul again, he lived "for the sake of the gospel" (1 Cor 9:23). Chastity is evangelical. Chastity moves our hearts and minds to an awareness of dependency on God. Chastity is trusting God. Celibate chastity is an ability to say God is enough. But, of course, God is not enough. We all want God and more besides, but chastity is trusting that what we need in our personal and interpersonal lives God will provide. Chastity, like all the vows, is an act of faith in a God who loves. Chastity is also essential to a shared life in common. It too is a path to holiness.

---

22. Bede Jarrett, OP, *The Life of St. Dominic* (Westminster, MD: The Newman Bookshop, 1947), 173.

St. Paul instructed the Corinthians, who had their own issues with chastity: "Love is patient; love is kind; love is not envious or boastful or arrogant or rude" (1 Cor 13:4). Chastity is learning how to love, and if Aquinas is right in describing hope as leaning on God,[23] so is chastity: learning to lean on God and on others. Chastity makes us aware of our dependence on others. We can't go it alone in life. Once again, St. Paul shows us his particular love for the Philippians when he writes them:

> I thank my God whenever I think of you; and every time I pray for all of you, I pray with joy, remembering how you have helped to spread the Good News from the day you first heard it right up to the present. I am quite certain that the One who began this good work in you will see that it is finished when the Day of Christ Jesus comes. It is only natural that I should feel like this towards you all, since you have shared the privileges which have been mine: both my chains and my work defending and establishing the gospel. You have a permanent place in my heart, and God knows how much I miss you all, loving you as Christ Jesus loves you. My prayer is that your love for each other may increase more and more and never stop improving your knowledge and deepening your perception so that you can always recognize what is best. This will help you to become pure and blameless, and prepare you for the Day of Christ, when you will reach the perfect goodness which Jesus Christ produces in us for the glory and praise of God. (Phil 1:3–11)[24]

---

23. Thomas Aquinas, *Summa Theologiae*, II–II, q. 17, a. 1.
24. The translation for this text and the following one comes from *The Jerusalem Bible*.

One can picture Dominic praying with this reading from St. Paul. One can envision it shaping his words as he takes leave of his brethren or sisters on varied occasions. Neither St. Paul nor St. Dominic would be embarrassed about their particular affection for someone or for a particular community. It was a part of a healthy chaste life. Paul went on to say to the Philippians: "I miss you very much, dear friends; you are my joy and my crown" (Phil 4:1), and also:

> I want you to be happy, always happy in the Lord; I repeat, what I want is your happiness. Let your tolerance be evident to everyone: the Lord is very near. There is no need to worry, but if there is anything you need, pray for it, asking God for it with prayer and thanksgiving, and that peace of God, which is so much greater than we can understand, will guard your hearts and your thoughts in Christ Jesus. Finally, brothers, fill your minds with everything that is true, everything that is noble, everything that is good and pure, everything that we love and honor, and everything that can be thought virtuous or worthy of praise. Keep doing all the things that you learn from me and have been taught by me and have heard or seen that I do. Then the God of peace will be with you. (Phil 4:4–9)

As it was for St. Paul, so it was for St. Dominic. The chaste life is about love. Chastity is about loving someone in particular but not possessively. Like poverty, it is about being, not about having. With poverty it is not having or being possessed by things, while with chastity it is not having or being possessed by persons. It is a nonaddictive way of being in the world. It means, in other words, true freedom, deepening one's capacity to love. It cherishes both the call to serve and also the gift of friendship. Dominic never saw his desire to go with William to preach to unbelievers as a violation of either chastity or obedience. The desire to preach was at the heart of both of them, but in the end he always surrendered to what was asked of him.

A HOLY PREACHING

Dominic's contemplative heart, love of learning, commitment to mendicant life, and his missionary spirit all show up in what contemporary Dominicans refer to as the four pillars of Dominican life: prayer, study, the common life, and preaching.[25] If known for anything, Dominic would have been known as a man of prayer. Stories abound of his spending entire nights in the chapel, or first visiting the Blessed Sacrament upon arriving at a destination, or the well-remembered line of instruction to his brothers to speak only about God or with God. The Liturgy of the Hours, the Prayer of the Church, was personal prayer for him, and his personal prayer was always praying with the Church.

Dominic also remained a lifelong student. Jordan described him as untiring and unremitting in his desire for study (*Libellus*, no. 7). As early as the summer of 1215, he attended the lectures of Alexander Stavensby with his first companions. He sent his preaching friars to great university centers for the education they would receive as well as for the education they would offer. Hence, the popularity of one of Fra Angelico's artistic depictions of Dominic sitting at the foot of the cross with a book, presumably the Scriptures (perhaps his beloved manuscript of the

---

25. I give a different twist to an approach to the four pillars in "The Pillars Revisited, A Fresh Look at Dominican Spirituality," *Spirituality* 13, no. 73 (July/August 2007): 192–99.

Gospel of Matthew) on his lap. Dominic was committed to a life of learning in the pursuit of truth. That is why he felt the need for his friars to be well educated, why a convent's lector is an important role in each community, why later the Order sent the most capable of its men to become masters at the University of Paris.

Dominic's spirit of brotherhood (*fraternitas*) and capacity for friendship manifests itself in yet another pillar of the Order, which we can name in various ways—the regular life, the common life, community life—each of which carries a significant nuance. Equally untiring was his love for the brethren. We can only speculate why it was Dominic that Bishop Diego had chosen. It becomes quite clear that a bond formed between them, or was deepened in their travels and eventually in a common mission. His capacity for friendship is something to which we have already referred. Dominic had already begun to learn something about human love through God's love and something of God's love through human love. Relationships remained significant for him throughout his life, while at the same time the monastic practices he relished in his life at Osma undergirded those relationships. But it was the preaching, the "Holy Preaching," to which all the other pillars pointed. Dominic was destined by the circumstances of his life and times, by a papal vision for the Church, and by the workings of divine providence for a task at hand. As his mother had given birth, so had he.

There are many facets to the Order Dominic founded, those that he inaugurated and those that emerged more and more clearly from the seeds he planted. I refer here to the intellectual traditions, the artistic traditions, the mystical traditions, the liturgical tradition, the apostolic tradition, and a missionary spirit. All of these can be found in Dominic himself, although they emerge with greater prominence here or there, now and then.

There was a mistaken notion in the latter part of the twentieth century that the Order Dominic founded was transformed or even refounded in light of the eventual reputation of Thomas Aquinas, who still stands as the greatest exemplification of the Order's intellectual history. Those who endorsed this point of view have seen the Order emphasize teaching more than preaching, scholarship more than simplicity of life, and Thomism more than the gospel itself. I do not see this discontinuity in the Order's history. Thomas himself undoubtedly understood that preaching alone was insufficient to undercut the Cathars, that the inquisition could not be the way of the future, and that only *sacra doctrina* would defeat the Manichees. In the legendary story about Aquinas's presence as a guest at a banquet of King Louis IX of France, Thomas was reported to have startled others at the banquet as from within the midst of meditative musings, he slammed on the table shouting, "And that will settle the Manichees!" He perhaps realized at that moment that Aristotle's philosophy would be more of an asset in undermining Manicheism and Catharism than Plato's philosophy, which was so prominent at the time, and hence he was even more resolved to put it at the service of the Holy Teaching.[26]

Dominic wanted his brothers to be both learners and teachers. He would have been pleased with Master Albert of Cologne, who was a theologian, a philosopher, a mystic, a professor, a contemplative, a provincial, and a reluctant bishop. These "traditions" in the Order are not so easily separated. Aquinas was drawn against his family's will to join the Order because he was inspired

---

26. G. K. Chesterton, *Saint Thomas Aquinas* (New York: Doubleday & Co., 1956), 97–101.

by its ideals. Dominic would have been proud to see one of his brothers occupy a chair in the faculty of theology at the University of Paris. Preaching required learning, and what one learned had to be shared. Dominic knew this from the beginning, and thus the early Chapters before Dominic's death already legislated that each convent had to have its teacher, its lector, whose classes all were required to attend, including the prior.

It is true that for Dominicans, for Dominic, learning and study were not an end in themselves but were geared toward a new evangelization. It is true in the beginning that the Order did not value secular learning but rather theological wisdom.[27] That gradually changed as one came to see that we cannot have one without the other. In this regard, Albert the Great, a naturalist and philosopher of nature, what we would call today a natural scientist, contributed to widening the ambience of the learning that was needed in order to preach or to have a theology that responded to the needs of the world. Early on, the brothers realized that following after Dominic did not necessarily mean something slavish, wearing the same kind of sandals that Dominic wore or, rather, chose not to wear when outside a town. Dominic is reported to have traveled on foot and without shoes but to avoid attention put shoes on when entering a town or village. Rather, it is for a Dominican to be for his or her period of history what Dominic was for his—someone who proclaims with integrity the Word of God as received from the Church. Learning does not take us further from the heart of the gospel but more deeply into it.

The same must be said of the Order's artistic traditions. Dominican art is a form of preaching. At a time when most

27. For the early history and development of study in the Order, see M. Michèle Mulchahey, *First the Bow is Bent in Study...Dominican Education before 1350* (Toronto, Canada: Pontifical Institute of Medieval Studies, 1998).

Catholics did not read, they could 'read' a stained glass window or be called to an appreciation of the faith through a painting or chant. Architecture can communicate God's word also. Aquinas himself was also a poet.[28] Art has to do with beauty, with the senses, sound and sight. Beauty may bring home what words cannot convey. It can stir the heart as well as the mind. That is another level of the integration that preaching seeks: the union of heart and mind. Learning is arrogant when it separates the head from heart knowledge, and art can become mere sentimentality when it separates the heart from the mind. Dominic was not sentimental. He learned life as we all do, during a famine in Palencia, or during a time of war in the Languedoc, or upon separation from a friend.

The paintings and frescoes of the Dominican artist Fra Angelico (Brother John of Fiesole) have endured the test of time because they verge on the sublime.[29] Art is intended to lift the heart and mind to God. A friend of mine described his Dominican vocation as "loving God with his mind." This seems an apt description of Dominic, someone who loved God with his mind. And an artist might say something similar given his or her gifts; they are called to love God with their hands or voice. As Aquinas notes in his theology, we come to God through creation, to the cause from seeing the effects. Dominic remembered God by seeing God's handiwork in nature. Dominic walked and saw the beauty of the world, its flowering plants, its change of seasons, the plight of the poor, and the reality of leprosy. To preach

---

28. See Paul Murray, OP, *Aquinas at Prayer: The Bible, Mysticism and Poetry* (London: Bloomsbury, 2013), 157–259.

29. There are many works on Fra Angelico. See Jacqueline and Maurice Guillaud, *Fra Angelico: The Light of the Soul* (New York: Clarkson N. Potter, 1986), for a brief introduction to his life and works as well as excellent reproductions of the paintings and frescoes from the convent of San Marco, Florence.

with one's mind and with one's heart, with one's hands and one's voice, to glorify God in the body, as St. Paul put it (1 Cor 6:20).

We need not draw out these varied facets of the life of St. Dominic in further detail. Dominic was pictured as studious in *St. Dominic Reading a Book*, a detail from the fresco by Fra Angelico titled *The Mocking of Christ*.[30] Yet Dominic is also often depicted as standing before the crucifix in a meditative contemplation of the Passion of Christ. Thought, prayer, and art come together, and the Eucharist, then as now, was the source and summit of what it was all about.[31] Although, to my knowledge, we don't have paintings of Dominic presiding at Mass, it is worthwhile to form a picture for oneself. As much as the Eucharist was at the center of his life, how did he approach its celebration? What kind of reverence did he manifest? Was it then especially that he prayed for sinners? Did he experience rapture while at Mass? He is reported to have frequently been moved to tears while celebrating: "one tear would not wait for the next."[32] This is not pictured in the nine ways but undoubtedly would have been a powerful way of prayer for him. When he said the words of dismissal (*Ite, missa est,* "Go, the Mass is ended), did he envision all the apostolic and missionary efforts in which his friars were engaged? Did he not, as much as any, realize that the contemplation needed to culminate in the handing on of its fruits? Was he not at heart both a contemplative man and a missionary?

Perhaps we can hold out before us the portrait that the nineteenth-century Dominican Henri Lacordaire, OP, held up upon his reestablishing the Order in France:

---

30. In the Museum of San Marco, Florence.
31. Vatican II, *Lumen Gentium*, no. 11.
32. Vicaire, *Saint Dominic and His Times*, 24.

If eloquence is the most difficult of all the arts, and if preaching is the highest of all kinds of eloquence, then it is no small phenomenon to see one single man suddenly producing an army of preachers which could shake up people everywhere from Spain to Muscovy, from Sweden to Persia. To explain this extraordinary fact it is enough to bear in mind that eloquence is the daughter of passion. Create a passion in a soul, and eloquence will gush forth from it in torrents. Eloquence is the sound which a passionate soul makes. This is why hosts of orators are born in times of public unrest, when peoples are stirred by powerful interests. And whoever has loved anything intensely at any time in his life has inevitably been eloquent, even if only once. So St. Dominic had no need to found schools of rhetoric in order to send legions of preachers into the world; all he needed was to touch the very heart of his age and to find there or awaken there a passion.[33]

MARY, PATRONESS OF THE PREACHING FRIARS

We have already spoken often of two of the mottos of the Order: Truth (*Veritas*) and "To contemplate and to hand on to others the fruits of one's contemplation" (*Contemplari et contemplata aliis tradere*). The latter are words from Thomas Aquinas. The former was at the heart of the preaching, although as a motto for the Order it came later.[34] We have not yet referred to the third motto—"to praise, to bless, to preach" (*laudare, benedicere,*

---

33. Henri Lacordaire, OP, *Essay on the Re-establishment in France of the Order of Preachers*, ed. and trans. Simon Tugwell, OP (Dublin: Dominican Publications, 1983), 22.
34. See Guy Bedouelle, OP, *Saint Dominic: The Grace of the Word*, trans. Sister Mary Thomas Noble, OP (San Francisco: Ignatius Press, 1987), 168.

praedicare). *To praise*—as Dominic did and the whole Church does in its Liturgy of the Hours, and all of creation also does. *To bless*—as Dominic's life was a blessing, in whose presence others felt blessed. This is what preaching is intended to be: to proclaim good news. Hence, the Scripture text most often used as a first reading for the Feast of St. Dominic when celebrated as a solemnity: "How beautiful are the feet of one who brings good news, bears glad tidings of salvation" (Isa 52:7–10). Of course, the focus of it all is *to preach*, but how the motto came to be tells a story as well.

Evidently, Conrad, the bishop of Prato, was coming through Bologna and found himself staying at the convent of the Friars Preachers. He, perhaps prudently, was concerned about the legitimacy of this motley crew with its innovative perspective on religious life. Thus, upon coming to choir, he asked if he might see a holy book, such as some might still do with the Bible today. The missal that was used at Mass was brought to him and he opened it up spontaneously to whatever page the Lord might speak to him. And on the top of the page were the words *Laudare, benedicere, et praedicare*—"to praise, to bless, to preach." God had spoken. It was enough reassurance for the bishop to know that he had been wisely guided to this holy house. In its own way, providence provided its blessing. But there is more. The words were on the page of the preface for a feast of the Blessed Mother. She was already assuming her role as protectress of the Order.

An equally interesting story further reflects the close link between a preaching friar and the Blessed Mother—how the *Salve Regina* came to be sung in houses after Night Prayer. A later legend attributes our Blessed Mother giving the rosary to St. Dominic, but the history of the rosary is another story. The Dominicans' deep association with it only emerges a century or so after Dominic.[35] Nevertheless, Dominic trusted Mary in his prayer from the beginning. It so happened, sometime after Dominic's death, that a brother in Bologna came to be possessed by a demon that plagued the community, including Brother Jordan. While preparing one day to say Mass, Jordan recited Psalm 34, and during his prayer, the demon's wickedness was exposed. In gratitude for the work of the demon being brought out into the open, the community was prompted "for the first time to sing the *Salve Regina* after Compline at Bologna, and this practice spread from there to the rest of the province of Lombardy, and finally the same devout and beneficial practice was adopted throughout the whole Order" (*Libellus*, no. 120). To Mary, and to Mary Magdalene, as well as to Catherine of Alexandria, the Order was entrusted, witnessing Dominic's own appreciation of the role that women had played in his own life. As Mary gave birth to the Word in her womb, so the Preacher gives birth to the Word in the world. As Augustine, Aquinas, Eckhart, and others have indicated, before Mary could give birth to the Word in her womb, she had to give birth to the Word in her heart. Likewise the Preacher, before giving birth to the Word for others, needs to give birth to the Word in his or her own heart.

Tradition holds that the dispersal of the brethren in 1217 took place on the Feast of the Assumption. In 1218, our Blessed Mother appeared to Brother Reginald in conjunction with the

---

35. The common impression that the rosary was given to St. Dominic himself by our Blessed Mother is mistaken, although Dominic himself did have a devotion to Mary. The practice of praying the *Aves* and *Pater Nosters*, of course, had a history as does the rosary itself. Alan de la Roche, OP (1428–75), in the fifteenth century, played a significant role in attributing the invention of the rosary to St. Dominic. The rosary was added to the habit of the friars in the sixteenth century. See Guy Bedouelle, OP, *Saint Dominic, The Grace of the Word*, 253–57, for a brief discussion. For a more extensive discussion of the history of the rosary, see Anne Winston-Allen, *Stories of the Rose, The Making of the Rosary in the Middle Ages* (University Park, PA: The Pennsylvania State University Press, 2005).

cure that followed upon the prayer of Dominic. Dominic himself had a vision of Mary. In an account given by Sister Cecilia, who heard of it from Dominic himself, Dominic saw our Lord and his Blessed Mother, in whose presence he saw religious of every order but none from among his own preaching friars. Dominic wept at the sight. Christ inquired of Dominic why he wept and Dominic answered, "Because I see members of every religious Order but none of my own." Christ replied, "I have given over your Order to my mother's care." At this Mary drew back her mantle and opened it wide, and Dominic saw that the mantle enclosed within it a multitude of his own preaching friars.[36]

If a saint is someone who makes others want to be saints, then Dominic was indeed a saint. He seems to have spoken intensely with God and eloquently about God and still speaks to us of God today. As an active contemplative, a contemplative itinerant, a mendicant who begged for food and begged God for mercy, a preacher of grace, a preaching friar, he was someone who loved God with his whole heart and his neighbor as if she were his very self. He was a friend of God who befriended others and eventually an Order of Preachers.

> *Praedicator gratiae, nos junge beatis.*

> "Preacher of grace, unite us with the blessed."
> —From an antiphon in honor of St. Dominic

---

36. *Lives of the Brethren*, 81–83, from the *Miracula of Blessed Cecilia*, no. 7.

SUGGESTIONS FOR FURTHER READING

Bedouelle, Guy. *Saint Dominic: The Grace of the Word*. Translated by Sister Mary Thomas Noble. San Francisco: Ignatius Press, 1987. A very accessible read by a competent Dominican scholar who not only gives us the life of Dominic but also insights into his spirituality.

Hinnebusch, William A. *The Dominicans, A Short History*. Dublin: Dominican Publications, 1985.

———. *The History of the Dominican Order*. 2 vols. Staten Island, NY: Alba House, 1966, 1973. A valuable resource with a wealth of information.

Jordan of Saxony. *On the Beginnings of the Order of Preachers*, the *Libellus*. Translated by Simon Tugwell. Dublin: Dominican Publications, 1982. Also available in a translation by R. F. Larcher, in *Saint Dominic: Biographical Documents*. Edited by Francis Lehner. Washington, DC: The Thomist Press, 1964.

Koudelka, Vladimir J. *Dominic*. Translated by Consuelo Fissler and Simon Tugwell. London: Darton, Longman and Todd Ltd., 1997. A very readable introduction to the life of Dominic and selected pertinent texts.

McGonigle, Thomas, and Phyllis Zagano. *The Dominican Tradition*. Collegeville, MN: The Liturgical Press, 2006.

Murray, Paul. *The New Wine of Dominican Spirituality: A Drink Called Happiness*. London: Burns and Oates, 2006.

O'Meara, Thomas F., and Paul Philibert. *Scanning the Signs of the Times: French Dominicans in the Twentieth Century*. Adelaide, Australia: AFT Ltd., 2013.

Philibert, Paul, OP, "Roman Catholic Prayer: The *Novem modi orandi sancti Dominici*," in *Contemplative Literature: A Comparative Sourcebook on Meditation and Contemplative Prayer*, ed. Louis Komjathy (Albany, NY: State University of New York Press, 2015), 503–45.

preachingfriars.org. A website of the student brothers of the Central Province of Dominican Friars, the Province of St. Albert the Great, and the Southern Province, the Province of St. Martin de Porres.

Radcliffe, Timothy. *I Call You Friends*. New York: Continuum, 2001. While not explicitly about things Dominican, this collection of intensely personal writings by the former Master of the Order of Preachers is suffused with Dominican spirituality.

Tugwell, Simon, ed. *Early Dominicans*. Classics of Western Spirituality. New York: Paulist Press, 1982. Selected writings with an excellent introduction by Simon Tugwell.

———. "Notes on the Life of St. Dominic." In *Archivum Fratrum Praedicatorum*. Rome: Istituto Storico Domenicano, vol. 65 (1995), 5–169; vol. 66 (1996), 5–200; vol. 67 (1997), 27–59; vol. 68 (1998), 5–116; vol. 73 (2003), 5–141. Tugwell has provided us with some of the most recent research. Unfortunately, much of it is less accessible and only available in the volumes from the Historical Institute of the Order of Preachers. I have thus availed myself of this research in the present book in order to make it more available.

————. *The Way of the Preacher*. London: Darton, Longman and Todd Ltd., 1979.

Vicaire, Marie-Humbert. *The Genius of St. Dominic*. Nagpur, India: Dominican Publications, n.d. A collection of essays.

————. *Saint Dominic and His Times*. Translated by Kathleen Pond, a translation of the first edition. New York: McGraw-Hill Book Co., 1964. Reprinted by Alt Publishing Co., Green Bay, Wisconsin. Remains an unsurpassed authoritative work, although some interpretations are now dated.

Vidmar, John. *Praying with the Dominicans*. New York: Paulist Press, 2008.

Woods, Richard. *Mysticism and Prophecy: The Dominican Tradition*. London: Darton, Longman and Todd Ltd., 1998.

Advance Praise for *St. Dominic*

"The ease with which Fr. Donald Goergen, OP, presents the life of St. Dominic, often not well known to many, allows the reader to enter the contemplative life of a man who flourishes through his friendship with God and others within the context of his times. Fr. Donald presents the historical context of St. Dominic clearly and simply so the reader can see our holy founder's life unfold in a joyful obedience, a listening, from which he courageously followed the road set out for him in Divine Providence that formed him as a preacher of grace, beginning with his family in Caleruega and ending with his new family, his community, gathered around him as he prepared to enter communion with God and the saints. Any reader will take away from this book a better understanding of St. Dominic and, it is hoped, a renewed obedience, that is, a contemplative listening to the grace of God at work in all of us."

—Fr. Bruno Cadoré, OP, Master of the Order

"This readable book offers insights into how St. Dominic's localized band of preachers became an international religious order, revolutionary in its structure and scope. The description of the earliest days of the Dominicans, both men and women, and the challenge by the popes to Dominic to think beyond the Languedoc region of France are especially informative."

—John Vidmar, OP, associate professor of history,
Providence College, RI, and author of
The Catholic Church Through the Ages (Paulist Press)

"Fr. Donald Goergen's book brings a fresh approach to a familiar tale by combining serious historical research with the personal insights of a man who has labored hard and long, preaching the gospel in the steps of St. Dominic.

—Sr. Barbara Beaumont, OP, Fanjeaux, France